BUCKLE UP, FRIENDS!

In *The Sorry Syndrome,* Dr. John Waterhouse shakes you out of a comfort zone that for so many has become an insidious confinement zone. He brilliantly guides us through a fresh, exciting, and revolutionary way to embrace personal responsibility, helping us see that blame and apology are about the past. When we break free of the Sorry Syndrome and become fully present, then understanding, communication, and learning flourish. It's a powerful step into a life of growth and joy!

— BRIAN BIRO
America's Breakthrough Coach

THE
SORRY
SYNDROME

How to Learn from Missteps
Without Apologizing

JOHN B. WATERHOUSE, PhD

Park Point
PRESS

573 Park Point Drive
Golden, Colorado 80401-7042

Park Point Press
573 Park Point Drive
Golden, Colorado 80401-7402

Printed in the United States of America
Published December 2016

COVER DESIGN & BOOK LAYOUT MARIA ROBINSON, DESIGNS ON YOU, LLC
LITTLETON, COLORADO 80121

ISBN e-book: 978-0-917849-57-2
ISBN: 978-0-917849-56-5

I'm sorry, so sorry

That I was such a fool

I didn't know love could be so cruel

You tell me mistakes are part of being young

But that don't right the wrong that's been done

I'm sorry, so sorry

Please accept my apology

But love is blind, and I was too blind to see

— Lyrics from
"I'm Sorry"
by Brenda Lee

CONTENTS

ACKNOWLEDGMENTS

Nothing is more important in my life than acknowledging the powerful presence of my wife and life partner, Dr. Barbara Waterhouse. No one else has ever believed in me the way she does. No one else has ever loved me as unconditionally as she does. Through the ups and downs of life, she has always been there for me like no one else. Thank you, Barbara, for staying by my side through the extraordinary journey of our lives together. The best is yet to come.

I must also acknowledge with great gratitude my Native American teacher, Will Rockingbear. Over the years, Rockingbear's teachings about the ancient ways of North America's original inhabitants have greatly influenced my life. It was he who first pointed out to me the flawed concept of being sorry. This idea has never left me—and certainly never will. Thank you, Rockingbear, for being my good teacher in this physical realm—and beyond.

Finally, I acknowledge my first life teacher, Ken Dyers. During my short time with him in Sydney, Australia, he taught me to harness the power we wield through life on planet Earth and that everyone who embraces their inner power can make an extraordinary difference in the world. Ken once said to me that if I was going to make a mistake, I should make a big one; this way, whatever I learned from it would bring significant meaning and value into my life. This radical idea may sound humorous, but it's always stayed with me, helping me make the most of my missteps.

To everyone else who has touched my life along the way, you have all contributed to a life that has grown only fuller, richer, and more valuable throughout the years.

My life is an overflowing abundance of blessings!

A quiet and insidious epidemic pervades the human experience. It's a transcultural attempt to simplify our lives, but it's not working. We incessantly show the symptoms of this disease with no understanding of its meaning or the negative outcomes it creates in our lives.

I call this condition the Sorry Syndrome. People across the planet are continually infecting each other with the idea that saying "I'm sorry" somehow corrects their socially clumsy and inappropriate actions and appeases those they think they've offended.

Most of us feel obligated to utter these two words whenever there's even the slightest chance we've offended someone. Such a reaction often goes unnoticed by others. But by being so repetitive, it becomes an insincere, superficial, and unconscious gesture that has no meaning. Worse yet, it holds us in a pattern of thinking we can apologize for anything at any moment—and that's the end of it.

The bottom line is, "I'm sorry" doesn't get us where we want to go. In fact, it takes us in the wrong direction.

For some, "I'm sorry" comes from a sense of personal inadequacy. People use this phrase to apologize on cue because they have extremely low opinions of themselves. I did this at an earlier time in my life, but I overcame that tendency. I became more willing to recognize and embrace a higher understanding of my inherent value as a person. It was incredibly liberating to find that my life has meaning and purpose—and it isn't an endless stream of screwups!

The bigger issue for most people is that when they say, "I'm sorry," they don't learn anything; they don't become more conscious of how their thinking influences their sense of self. They aren't aware of how these two little words pull them down every time they leave their mouths. When people speak these two words, they're in a state of denial, at best. At worse, they're consciously lying to themselves—and everyone in their lives.

Being sorry has become chronic—and it's getting worse. When people don't like what others say or do, they expect them to say they're sorry. Apologies have become an unhealthy—and toxic—cultural norm.

People don't just say "sorry" to one another; machines say it to us all the time. We program our phone systems to say things like, "I'm sorry, that's not a working number" or "I'm sorry, there's no one at that extension." What! Machines are sorry? I don't think so!

Corporate America has adopted being sorry as standard company policy. Customer service agents are trained to start conversations by apologizing for things they didn't do. When I call them for support, I don't want them to be sorry. I want them to help me get what I want, which has nothing to do with being sorry.

Being sorry isn't a pleasantry or a courtesy. It's demeaning and ineffective. Worse yet, we've grown numb to its effect on our psyches.

Many people now interpret Yom Kippur, the Jewish High Holy Day of Atonement, as a day of apology. Hebrew tradition, however, directs people to use this day to forgive and make things right with their family members and friends. How did the idea of mandating contrition work its way into such a hallowed occasion?

The idea that being sorry isn't such a good thing became clear to me one day when I was sitting in a circle with Will Rockingbear, my Cherokee shaman teacher. I was a member of a group that gathered every Thursday at his lodge at the base of Mt. Mitchell, the tallest peak in the eastern United States. In our conversations that day, the subject of being sorry came up rather innocently.

Rockingbear was known for his economy of words; they were potent and memorable. His advice that day was true to form: "*I'm sorry* means I'm uncomfortable with your upset about what I did, so I'd like you to stop it. And, by the way, I'll probably do it again."

Rockingbear's words stunned me. He had given me the clearest understanding I'd ever experienced about the idea of being sorry. It completely resonated with me, and I wanted to find evidence to prove his perceptions. Since then, I've found plenty of proof (apparently enough for an entire book on the subject).

I offer this book to you as a way of rethinking your love affair with being sorry. But let me warn you—this isn't a book about getting people to forgive you when you mess up. It isn't about being oblivious and indifferent to the ways your words and actions impact others.

With this book, you can hone your social skills and modify your behavior. You can become more fully present—mentally and emotionally—in every aspect of your life. As you explore our cultural obsession with being sorry, you'll learn to be clear and centered with a deeper awareness of who you truly are. Join me in exploring this next step on our evolutionary path as co-inhabitants of planet Earth.

PART I

1

A CULTURE
OF BLAME, REMORSE, AND
DEFENSIVENESS

Something catastrophic happens: A passenger jet goes down, a mine caves in, or a levy collapses. One of a seemingly infinite number of possible scenarios occurs involving man-made structures or equipment. News reporters wait for a public official to brief them on the event. The official comes to the podium and says, "We find no evidence of human error."

What?! The members of the media are incensed. Someone must be at fault here—a person, company, or government agency to blame. Surely if we can identify the guilty party, we can begin the healing process. If we can assign blame for this terrible occurrence, we'll be so much better off. If we just knew who made this fatal error, we could focus our attention on them and everything would be okay, wouldn't it? We need a target, don't we? We need to know who did this so we can all rest safely at night . . . right?

Do you see how ludicrous this is? It's the mentality of a dysfunctional society, but we see it as just the way things are. We listen intently to news broadcasts and read newspapers, magazines, and blogs to find out who's at fault and who to blame for each terrible event.

For instance, a politician is accused of having an affair. He denies it. When someone brings evidence forward to confirm the accusations, he contritely admits he's strayed from the straight and narrow. He offers profound apologies to his wife, his family, his constituents, and (of course) to God. "Well," his supporters say, "he said he was sorry—that should be the end of it." Two years later, he's accused of similar behavior, and the whole scenario begins again. But this time, he's forced to resign from his elected position, forever disgraced.

The politician's supporters thought that because he said he was sorry, he'd automatically and permanently change his behavior. But why would he? He enjoyed what he was doing; it brought him pleasure. (However, pleasure didn't make his acts culturally acceptable.) Being sorry isn't a reliable predictor of lasting changes in people's conduct.

On the contrary, this politician's apology meant he was looking for an easy way out of a difficult situation. When he succeeded, he transgressed again. Of course, he was even sorrier when he got caught the second time. He may have had deep regrets, but he was far more regretful about being caught and called out in public than he was about disappointing anyone.

Imagine your doctor says you need to get an injection. As she inserts the needle into your skin and you wince, she says, "I'm sorry." But why would she possibly be sorry? She isn't sorry about giving you a shot; it was her idea! She certainly isn't sorry she gets to charge you for the medicine and her services. Is she sorry about it hurting a little? Why? She knows shots hurt. Does hearing her say that she's sorry take your pain away? It never has for me.

As we all do, your doctor says "I'm sorry" after even the smallest inconveniences and disruptions. People in our culture are addicted to instant blame (especially self-blame) and instant repentance. We say we're sorry and forgive each other (if we're in the mood) and move on. We position ourselves so people will like us and we can get what we want.

A woman pushing a shopping cart through the market comes up behind me and bangs into my heel with the front of her cart. "Ouch!" I bark.

"I'm sorry," she says.

"That doesn't stop the pain in my heel!" I retort.

Looking at me with great disdain, she pushes her cart past me in a huff muttering, "I said I was sorry!"

Moments later from the other end of the aisle, I hear, "Ouch!" and a familiar voice says, "I'm sorry."

You might think this woman has a mental disorder—and perhaps she does—but how many times have you and I reacted the same way? Haven't you ever said "I'm sorry" in an attempt to get your way, or be forgiven for inappropriate behavior, or avoid the consequences of your actions?

"I'm sorry" is a cop-out. It's an enormously overused social norm that's way out of control. We say it without reflecting on what we've done so that we can move on as if nothing had happened. I'm sorry . . . I'm sorry . . . I'm sorry . . .

There has to be a better way for us to take responsibility for our actions in a world where others won't always like or agree with our actions.

But before I share my ideas about a better way of living, I invite you to look more deeply into a subtle dilemma we face in the Sorry Syndrome.

REMORSE DOESN'T EQUAL LEARNING— LEARNING EQUALS LEARNING

When someone says "I'm sorry" or "I apologize," what do they actually mean? Imagine that you've been bumped, inconvenienced, distracted, dissatisfied, bothered, troubled, insulted, betrayed, forgotten, abused, or otherwise *done wrong*. The person who committed this inappropriate act looks at you and says, "Oh, I'm really, really sorry."

In that moment, do you feel satisfied? Maybe you do—but is this a valid and useful reaction? Has anything actually changed? What makes you let go of this perceived transgression? The person said he was sorry, so he must be sorry—right?

What does this actually mean? Other than fulfilling a cultural norm, what value does being sorry actually provide?

When people say "I'm sorry," they recognize you don't like what they did. They don't want you to hold this against them; however, they aren't saying they've learned anything from the experience. In fact, by saying "I'm sorry," they're all but assuring you they'll do it again, either to you or someone else. Uttering these two words certainly didn't correct the situation.

Of course, this contradicts what society would have us believe. In our culture, saying "I'm sorry" is an easy way out of uncomfortable situations. It's expected and almost always accepted. Nothing actually changes, however, when someone says, "I'm sorry."

I've learned from calling people out who say they're sorry. For example, a checkout clerk at a market asked me to sign a receipt. As she tried to put a pen on the counter, it fell from her hand onto the counter. It fell all of an inch, but she proclaimed, "Oh, I'm sorry." "What are you sorry about?" I asked. "I don't know," she replied. She didn't know because saying she's sorry is a mindless, unconscious auto-response. She's said *sorry* to people her entire life.

But why?

We don't learn to say we're sorry in the midst of serious, life-altering circumstances. We learn it from our early caregivers. When three-year-old Penny takes a toy away from three-year-old Wendy, Penny's mother says, "You give that toy back to Wendy and say you're sorry!"

After additional prompting (Penny isn't ignoring Mommy; she's processing the experience), Penny looks down, hands over the toy, and says, "I'm sorry, Wendy."

But is she sorry? Not really. She's upset she had to give the toy back and doesn't understand why. Facing her mother's upset is very unpleasant, however, and the humiliation of being scolded in front of others is a bigger trauma than any other part of this experience. Penny knows she can get out of this fix by doing as she's told and saying, "I'm sorry."

Penny resents Wendy for ending up with the toy and feels emotionally injured by this public reprimand. The only thing that helped was that when she said she was sorry (whether she meant it or not), her mother stopped making demands of her. As a result, she's learning to say she's sorry simply to avert emotional discomfort.

As children, we learn to escape blame by saying that we're sorry as quickly as possible. *Sorry* has become the quintessential neutralizer of unacceptable behavior. When we feel embarrassment and failure, we intrinsically anchor on the idea and expression of being sorry. It's as if someone flipped a switch or pushed a button wired to our psyche that instantly relieves discomfort. Much of the time, we don't even require a response from the other person. We said we were sorry; we want and expect that to be enough.

Sorry goes both ways. In this scenario, Wendy learned that when she's upset by another's actions, her protests will result in getting what she wants (the toy). With this action will come the words, "I'm sorry." She feels better when this happens and expects to hear these words whenever she's upset or unhappy.

Both of the children in this scenario learned response patterns. Their conditioning is similar to the famous Pavlov's Dog experiment, in which dogs heard a bell ring when they were given food. As a result, they developed an expectation of being fed whenever they heard a bell. Researchers verified this by ringing a bell without dispensing any food; the dogs still salivated, expecting a meal. In the same way, when a child gives back (or gets back) a toy and says (or hears) "I'm sorry," any upset is averted. They feel a sense of well-being. All of this reinforces their desire to speak or hear "I'm sorry" whenever conflicts arise.

NO HOLY EVIDENCE

Did Jesus ever say, "I'm sorry"? Did the Buddha encourage his followers to be sorry? What about the Prophet Muhammad or Lord Krishna? Have you ever heard of any enlightened master or avatar who exclaimed, "I'm sorry"?

Do any sacred scriptures contain the words *I'm sorry?* Are they written anywhere in the Holy Bible, the Torah, the Quran, the Bhagavad Gita, or the Tao Te Ching?

Nowhere in these ancient texts—these foundational writings of the world's great religions—is there any mention of remorse-fulness as a virtue.

The reason for this seems clear to me. All great thinkers have detractors. History's great teachers and the authors of the world's sacred texts must have offended and confused some of their contemporaries. Just like us, they had emotions and physical bodies, but they were far more likely to lose their lives as a result of offending the sensibilities of others or challenging the status quo. These historical figures spoke of sorrow, pain, and suffering; however, being sorry appears not to have been a cultural norm in ancient times.

It's possible that people abased themselves to authority figures—especially when on the wrong side of power. But they don't seem to have had any phraseology for simply eliminating their wrong actions. There weren't any bankruptcy courts, only indentured servitude; perhaps these people didn't have any opportunities to be sorry. When people resolved mistakes through public stoning and other forms of execution, this left little room for human error.

If our religious texts don't say it's important or meaningful to burden ourselves with regret, why do we do it?

Jesus told his followers to shine their light into the world for all to see. That's a much better way to live than ever being sorry.

THE ORIGINS OF SORRY

According to my etymological sources, the word *sorry* was first recorded around 1250 CE, during Europe's Protestant Reformation. The word *sorry* comes from the Germanic word *sairaz* (physical or mental pain) and the Old English word *sarig* (distressed and full of sorrow). It's also directly related to the Old English word *sar* (wretched, worthless, and poor). Over time, *sar* evolved into the word sore. (Plato's *Phaedo*, trans. E. Brann, P. Kalkavage, E. Salem. Indianapolis: Focus Publishing, 1998).

When we're sorry, we claim pain and distress into our lives. We create feelings of wretchedness, worthlessness, and poverty. These consequences should be enough motivation for us to give up our addiction to the insipid idea of being sorry.

Experts first recorded the expression *I'm sorry* around 1834—less than 200 years ago! This idea didn't exist throughout the millennia of human existence; it's a relatively new concept. That's another excellent reason to drop it from our lexicon. We've tried it, and it just doesn't work.

Nonetheless, being sorry is a deeply ingrained cultural norm. Most people will want more evidence before simply letting it go and embracing something new. That's exactly what I offer in this book.

WHAT ABOUT APOLOGIZING INSTEAD?

At this point you may be thinking, "Okay, I'll never say I'm sorry again. Instead, I'll say, 'I apologize,'" which means you'll defend your actions and attempt to justify them. That's the original definition of *apologize*. It means that what happened was exactly what you intended, and it's an explanation of why you stand by what you said or did.

The word *apology* originated in the early fifteenth century. It's synonymous with defense and justification and comes from the Latin and Greek words *apologia* (a defense) and *apologeisthai* (to speak in one's defense). Therefore, according to its original meaning, apologizing isn't an effective alternative to being sorry.

If you're feeling a bit overwhelmed by all this, don't worry. There's a viable alternative to saying you're sorry, which I'll describe soon. First, however, I want to offer you a deeper understanding of the Sorry Syndrome.

2

WHY
SORRY DOESN'T
WORK

It's not that we don't enjoy saying we're sorry. Normal, healthy adults don't want to offend others or infringe on their well-being—even in the most insignificant ways. "I'm sorry" automatically falls out of our mouths faster than spit. We know people expect this response, and we think it helps. We really just want everything to be all right.

All of this is why—for me—being sorry doesn't work. We say it, but we don't mean it. The truth is, it isn't in our nature to be sorry. We're magnificent spiritual beings who incarnated on this planet to awaken—that's our nature. Being sorry takes us to a place of "less than." It implies we're innately wrong and means we've transgressed a social law. Apologizing means we're flawed beings who've fallen short of who we've come here to be. This just isn't true.

Instead of taking my word for this, consider for a moment that you—as a spiritual being—are perfect, whole, and complete. Yes, you—but not just you. Imagine everything and everyone around you as perfect, whole, and complete. What a concept!

We live in a perfect universe. Yes, I mean *perfect!* My definition of perfect, however, may be a little different from yours. Many people see life as right/wrong and good/bad; they perceive it as perfect only when their experiences exactly align with their expectations—which drastically limits their perspective. Who (other than that critical voice in our head) ever said our expectations must dictate the way things are?

When someone falls and breaks a bone, that break is perfect. It aligns perfectly with the laws of the physical universe. Given the events that occurred in that person's life, that break is the only thing that could have happened. Similarly, everything in an individual's consciousness that results from this broken bone is perfect. Our consciousness initiates our actions, which result in the circumstances and situations of our lives, even when those outcomes appear inconvenient and unwanted. We are at the core of everything that happens in our lives—from broken bones to broken hearts.

Here's an example of what I mean. Years ago on a Saturday night, a woman I knew fell in her apartment and injured her leg. So she called a close friend who came over immediately and drove her to a nearby hospital.

These two women believed in the power of prayer. While they waited in an emergency room, the woman who had come to help prayed for her friend's instantaneous healing. When the medical technicians took X-rays of the injured woman's leg, they didn't find a break. Both women were delightfully surprised. But as a precaution the ER doctor had her return the next Monday, and this time the X-ray revealed a break in the woman's leg. How did this happen? Had the woman's leg been broken all along? Or had it healed momentarily and then returned to being broken? No one knows.

What occurred next, however, is even more astounding. Stuck in a full leg cast, the injured woman needed round-the-clock help and having no other reasonable options, she moved in with her mother. Over the next six weeks, mother and daughter—living in close quarters—healed years of estrangement.

The broken leg was perfect in that it was the perfect facilitator of this major relationship healing. Even prayer couldn't deter the woman and her mother from this greater, hidden outcome. Life works just like this, without regard for our expectations. When we take the time to see how everything fits together so perfectly, it's quite amazing.

Life constantly and consistently reflects our consciousness back to us. The way we perceive life inside ourselves is reflected perfectly all around us: our fears, judgments, and limiting thoughts. Individual consciousness isn't about being good or bad; it's the sum total of our beliefs, emotional states, and what we're actively thinking and feeling. When we're upset, we draw difficult experiences into our lives. When we're afraid, we attract frightening experiences. When we feel peaceful, we experience the peaceful side of life.

Our mental and emotional activity constantly attracts things into our lives. If you want something to show up in your life, the best way to make it happen is to worry about it. Worry is like wearing a flashing neon sign saying "Here I am—over here! Bring me that big problem I'm so worried about. Go ahead, hit me with it!"

Life responds equally (and in exact proportion) to everything we embrace and resist. A perfect flow of energy directs the elements of our experience; it shows up in relation to what we think, feel, and believe. There are no accidents; however, there *are* coincidences—but not in the way we might think.

When you call something a coincidence, you're saying two or more random acts have occurred; you believe these two unconnected occurrences have something in common. A more accurate way to experience a coincidence is to realize all of life (perfect, whole, and complete) coincides and matches up at every point. Coincidences are the natural state of being; however, we experience this perfect unfoldment only when we're open to seeing the perfection of life.

Saying we're sorry (or wanting someone else to say it to us) denies the perfection of our lives. We don't have to be happy about everything others say and do. But making them wrong is a very superficial way of experiencing life. By "making wrong" I mean judging the words or actions of others with whom we disagree. When we look beyond our unrealized expectations, we can see the interactive elegance of all our (and everyone else's) experiences.

Sadly, people can find it nearly impossible to release the idea of being wrong. They insist on living in a world governed by rightness and wrongness. If someone can't let go of being wrong, they can't stop saying they're sorry.

I'm not suggesting we stop displaying manners. But being sorry isn't a prerequisite to living in a civilized society. If you bump into someone, it's okay to say, "Excuse me." That's what you want anyway, isn't it? You want to be excused to move beyond this moment without anyone carrying any emotional baggage. Many of us, however, face the challenge of "sorry addiction." We find it hard to stop saying it in important moments because we say it every time there's a bump in the road.

We're here to express the beauty and awesomeness of life. We must honor all life by knowing ourselves, others, and everything else as integral to life's unfolding perfection. Whenever we find fault in ourselves (and other people), we deny the intrinsic value of all. We reject the opportunity to deepen our awareness of the wonder of life.

If, after bumping into someone, you simply say "I'm sorry" and move on, you won't notice the brilliant being of light standing before you. You'll miss the momentary blessing of connecting with another light being. What a waste!

Take a few seconds to acknowledge within yourself the perfection of the person before you and the dance of life that brought you together. When you do this, everything about your experience becomes richer, lighter, and more valuable. Namaste!

Some time ago, I was traveling through a large city airport. I was hurrying from one gate to another to make a tight connection. As I approached a moving walkway, two women stepped on ahead of me. The older of the two was holding a young child; the other was maneuvering a stroller filled with coats and purses. A sign on the wall at the entry point listed restrictions for use of the walkway; one rule clearly prohibited strollers.

At the end of the walkway, the older woman stepped off. But as the stroller came off, it tipped forward, dumping its contents right in the middle of the exit point. The second woman was startled and quickly attempted to put her belongings back in the stroller. I was only a few seconds from getting off; I had read the sign and knew their behavior was not *okay*. I stepped over their things and squeezed around them, knowing others weren't far behind us. As I helped them clear the way, I said (in an indignant tone of voice), "The sign says no strollers."

The woman said, "Oh!" while feverishly rearranging her things. The other woman looked at me and said, "She can't read."

I was stunned. I turned and walked on. All the way to my gate, I couldn't let go of this idea. The woman wasn't rude or self-absorbed. She hadn't broken any rules (at least not any she was aware of). She couldn't read. She didn't know.

It had been a long time since I'd even thought about the issue of adult illiteracy and there it was, right in my face. Finding fault in this woman (or her actions) wouldn't help me. There was a perfectly good reason why: she couldn't read. Her challenges were so much greater than mine. I'd been inconvenienced for a few seconds; she'd faced a lifetime of challenges because she couldn't read. I instantly moved into a state of gratitude for my understanding and use of written English. I was grateful for my education and my ability to write and share ideas through books and articles.

I didn't feel sorry for the woman with the stroller. In fact, I was particularly grateful she hadn't said she was sorry to me. She'd given me an opportunity to experience a deep state of gratitude for my life and the gifts of knowledge I receive daily.

Most people experience their lives as mundane; they seek only to get through each day as easily as possible. If this were our highest reality, what would be the point?

Every circumstance, situation, and experience holds within it an invitation for us to awaken to the highest and deepest meaning of life. Our journey is about becoming ever more aware of the blessings we give and receive all day, every day—as revealed through our open hearts and minds.

We use the tools of our senses to maneuver through our three-dimensional reality. But we must develop an awareness beyond our senses to know the ultimate truth:

Life—in, as, and through us—is perfect, whole, and complete.

I'm not suggesting we become indifferent to the results of our actions. On the contrary, we need to take complete responsibility for everything we do. If, however, we were always open to the blessings of life that constantly sparkle before us, we'd stay in a perpetual state of gratitude and joy.

We exist at a point of choice between two actions: (1) finding fault and expressing remorse (which separate us from each other) and, (2) being aware of the elegance of all life—as experienced and expressed by each of us. Our payoff for choosing the latter is greater than we could ever comprehend.

3

MY AWAKENING

Years ago, I lived in Houston, Texas. My next-door neighbor was a highly successful business executive. He was also quite an athlete, but had a kind and gentle spirit and kept his competitive nature in check. One day he invited me to play tennis at our neighborhood recreation center. Our game was to be nothing serious; he called it "just hitting the ball around." He'd played in several citywide amateur tennis tournaments. I, on the other hand, had long appreciated the game but was no more than a novice. Clearly, he just wanted to relax and hang out with me.

When we started hitting the ball back and forth, it quickly became evident how much better he was than me. I'm sure he slowed his game down considerably so I could return his serves. Still, I missed many of his shots—and each time I missed, all I knew to do was say, "I'm sorry."

My obvious intimidation soon turned into embarrassment—and my play deteriorated from bad to worse. My problem was clearly in my head, but I had no idea how to pull myself out of this deepening hole of despair. I sensed my neighbor's frustration—not with my poor level of play, but with my incessant apologies and self-degradation. At my lowest point, I served the ball while calling out "Sorry!" as soon as my racquet touched the ball. Every time I did this, my premature apologies proved prophetic.

I finally told my neighbor I had to go home. I left the court feeling dejected and humiliated. What a miserable experience.

At that time, I saw myself as a successful young entrepreneur. I ran my own company, which did several millions of dollars of business annually, and lived in a beautiful, upscale home with my wife and children. If anyone had asked me how my life was going, I would have said I was on top of the world. I was upwardly mobile and made lots of money. That's what was important—or so I thought.

The greater truth was, I said I was sorry a lot back then. I was married to someone who found a lot of fault in me. Although I know now this was mostly about her own insecurities, at the time, I bought into her ever-diminishing sense of me.

I found fault in myself almost every day. It didn't take much for apologies to fly out of my mouth. I now recognize this as a symptom of my exceedingly unhappy situation. The only way I knew to cope with my incredibly painful and discontented life was to see myself as wrong, perceive myself as a failure, and apologize incessantly.

I thought I was doing a good job of hiding my internal critic from most people in my life. My public persona was confident and capable. I had a gift for stepping into the unknown and taking risks. But on the inside, I wasn't sure how I fit into the world. In my professional life, I managed to shine most of the time, but in my personal life, I was profoundly insecure.

I had been raised to believe the fundamental Christian premise that I was born a sinner into this world, but if I professed my Christian faith, I'd be saved for eternity from my sinful nature. I have no issue with those who accept this, but it didn't work for me. Even though I did everything I'd been told to do to save myself, I still felt unsettled and unresolved about the state of my life.

Thoreau said, "The mass of men lead lives of quiet desperation" *(Walden)*. I felt so desperate at this point in my life that I continually said "I'm sorry" to cope with my sense of inadequacy; it was my crutch. I used it to get by because I knew—deep inside—I wasn't good enough. I wasn't the man people believed me to be.

Within a year of that tennis match with my good neighbor, my life collapsed into abject failure. My business closed, my house went into foreclosure, my marriage ended abruptly (at least in my mind), and I ran away from home. I escaped to the other side of the planet—Sydney, Australia—because it was as far as I could get from home. In this alternative English-speaking culture, I could easily blend in, disappear, and keep my despair and self-loathing to myself.

But then within days of arriving in Sydney, I met the man who would become my first spiritual teacher. He taught a series of ongoing self-awareness classes in downtown Sydney, and I attended every one I could. Many of his students became my friends, and my life soon changed dramatically. Through what I learned—and remembered deep within myself—I awakened to my true nature. Every day, my life got brighter and clearer.

One day, my new friends and I were sitting around a table after class when someone suggested we play tennis that Saturday. Others immediately chimed in, saying they'd love a day of clay-court tennis. But when they asked me to join them, I felt a panic attack coming on and I declined: "Oh no—no thank you." My new friends watched me regress into the embarrassed, humiliated, and very *sorry* state I'd been in the last time I'd played tennis.

My teacher overheard our conversation and observed my less-than-enthusiastic reaction. An astute spiritual teacher, he came over and joined us. Looking directly at me he asked, "Do you know the best way to win a tennis match?"

"No," I sheepishly replied.

"Here's what to do," he began. "Step out onto the court and *own* it. Own the entire surface of the court—not just on your side, but the whole court. Own the lines on the court and the clay surface. Own the net and the posts that hold it up. Own the ground beneath the court—all the way down to the center of the earth. Own the space above the court—out to the fence that surrounds it and all the way up into the heavens. Own the air in that space, including the air you and your opponent breathe. Own all the tennis balls, your racquet, and your opponent's racquet, too. Take complete ownership of *everything* involved in this experience—even the clothes you and your opponent are wearing.

Then, give your opponent permission to be in your space, use your racquet, wear your clothes, and breathe your air.

"Don't say anything out loud," he continued. "Let it all happen in your mind. Just know you're completely and unequivocally in control of your entire experience. You control everything that happens on the court. If your mind's clear about what I'm telling you, you'll win every time."

I was dazzled by the possibilities in what he said. I turned to my friends (who were all smiling) and said, "Okay, let's play some tennis."

As I left, I felt a broad range of ambiguous emotions. Still I knew I had something big to learn from this experience. I focused on finding clothes, shoes, and a racquet for my upcoming tennis experience.

As agreed, we met that Saturday morning at a tennis park just outside the city. My opponent was Trevor—a young, very accomplished player. As I stepped onto the court, I asked him to give me a moment. He knew exactly what I was doing—and gladly obliged. After doing precisely what my teacher had described, I turned back to him and said, "Okay, I'm ready."

He served, and I returned the ball. Again and again, we exchanged long volleys. My shot placements were incredibly accurate—I couldn't miss! A crowd gathered and cheered as I controlled the match. I don't know if Trevor was playing anywhere near his peak ability. I, however, was performing at the highest athletic level of my life.

The value of this experience had nothing to do with beating Trevor; it was all about being my best. I had lettered in three sports in high school, but none of my previous athletic experiences had ever felt like this. I left the court with an overwhelming sense of personal accomplishment—and an inner healing that changed my life forever. I had taken my life back. I felt whole—perhaps for the first time ever.

Some time later, when reflecting on my experiences in Houston and Sydney, I realized I had achieved a paradigm shift in consciousness. I had come to a new way of being in the world. In this place, there was absolutely no possibility of being sorry.

So, in my earlier tennis experience, did being sorry make me perform poorly?

Yes! If not the entire reason for my failure, this attitude was certainly an integral part of my psychological makeup at the time. Self-blame and remorse never lead to healthy mental states, even—and especially—in cultures that demand such things.

Does owning everything on a tennis court (or in any other challenging circumstance) guarantee victory over an opponent?

Not at all. But, as a psychological exercise, it definitely changes the playing field for me.

A year later when I returned from Australia to the States, my mom invited me to her company's annual Fourth of July picnic. Soon after we arrived, her colleagues organized a pickup volleyball game. As sometimes happens, one team ended up with all the jocks while the other team was made up of "desk jockeys." I was an unknown, so the latter team picked me. I saw by the grins on our opponents' faces that they must have been thinking, "We're going to crush these guys!"

Before the match, I asked my team to huddle up, and I gave them a quick lesson on owning a competitive match. They were fast learners and immediately embraced this strategy. The game was stunning—our team dominated our more athletic rivals. The better we did, the more frustrated and ineffective our competitors became. Whenever our team slipped up, all I had to say was, "Own it!" and the next point was ours. We won every match that day— what a surprise!

Professional athletes typically have high levels of ownership. When they go through slumps, they're paying attention to their problems, not their mastery of the game, which intensifies their problems. An athlete immersed in abject failure might say, "I'm sorry I let down my team—and my fans."

It can be hard for athletes to climb out of these deep holes of despair. The best way for them to reverse these downward spirals is to remember who they are in the world, why they do what they do, and how it feels when they're in the zone. With a clear awareness of how success feels, accomplished competitors can easily return to excellence.

I've used athletic examples to illustrate my point, but this idea holds true for all of us! No one comes into this human experience to be sorry. It's incongruous to think that being sorry helps us be who we've come here to be—it can only get in our way.

Being sorry makes our energies stagnate and become heavy burdens. It keeps us focused on the problem; however, the answers we seek are never in the problem. As Albert Einstein once said, "No problem can be solved from the same level of consciousness that created it." The "sorry" level of consciousness aligns with the level of our problems.

Being sorry keeps us connected to and focused on what we *don't* want. On one hand, we say we don't want poor conditions in our lives—we want them to go away. On the other hand—by being sorry—we cling to the behaviors that brought on these conditions in the first place. The easiest resolution to this dilemma is to simply *stop being sorry*.

Here's an example of how being sorry can keep someone from learning from their missteps. For some time, I shopped exclusively at a men's clothing store in my city. I was on a first-name basis with the store manager, Charles, and relied on his expertise with men's fashions. Charles was an amiable man and always gave me his full attention when I came into his store.

On a particular occasion, I wanted to gift my friend Eric with a new dress shirt but I couldn't go with him because of a scheduling conflict. When I explained this to Charles, he suggested I leave my credit card with him so Eric could come in and select the shirt he wanted. Charles said he would take care of it, so I gratefully left my card with him.

I told Eric that Charles would charge the gift to my credit card and then give him the card and the receipt to return to me the following day. But when Eric brought me the receipt, it showed that additional items had been charged to my card. When I asked Eric what had happened, he said that Charles had asked him if he needed anything else and a minor shopping spree had ensued.

My agreement about the use of my credit card was with Charles, not with my friend, and I didn't want to overreact. This was a matter of principle for me, not money. I presumed I just needed to communicate my instructions more clearly to Charles. So on my next visit to the store, I told him he hadn't kept his agreement with me. He became immediately contrite and apologized profusely. I said, "Wait a minute; I haven't even told you what happened."

He replied, "It doesn't matter. I just want everything to be okay with you."

I described what hadn't worked for me, and he assured me it would never happen again.

Two months later, my stepson needed a suit for an important event, but I wasn't able to take him shopping, so my wife agreed to go with him. I gave her my credit card and called Charles to remind him of our agreement—that the *only* thing to be charged was a suit for my stepson. He, in turn, reminded me of how sorry he was.

"Only one suit goes on my card," I insisted. "Not a suit and a belt, not a suit and a pair of shoes, not a suit and anything else—okay?"

"Okay!"

When I returned home that evening, three new silk shirts were hanging in my closet. When I asked my wife where they came from, she explained that she'd gotten them for me. "How did you pay for them?" I asked.

"Charles put them on your credit card," she explained.

The next day, my wife returned the shirts and I found another men's clothing store to patronize.

More than anything, my feelings were hurt because no matter how clearly I thought I was communicating, I could no longer trust this very nice man to keep his agreement with me. I don't think Charles was being devious—he just wasn't good at learning from his missteps. His method of making things right was simply to say he was sorry. As a result, he lost a good customer.

Most of us want things to go well. We say we're sorry as a shortcut to making things better and getting our relationships back on track. The only problem is, it doesn't work.

To gain a complete understanding of the Sorry Syndrome, you'll want to consider other social dynamics. We'll look at them next.

4

THE DRAMA TRIANGLE

Saying "I'm sorry" means different things to different people. Some people believe that when they say these magic words, they're promising not to repeat an offensive act. Others (who would never say this out loud) mean something very different by this phrase. To them, "I'm sorry" translates as, "Okay, you caught me—now please stop bugging me about it." They might also mean, "I didn't consider how this thing I said (or did) would offend you, so stop making me feel bad about it." Some people even believe apologizing for hurting people somehow evens the score.

We have little at stake with those we cut off in traffic, bump into with our grocery carts, or pass on the sidewalk. In these everyday interactions, our "sorries" carry little weight. However, in our valued relationships with friends, family, and coworkers, we want our "sorries" to have lasting effects on our senses of self, status in groups, and overall well-being. In intimate relationships, we all tell our partners we're sorry once in a while.

The psychological model known in Transactional Analysis as the Karpman Drama Triangle (developed by Stephen B. Karpman, M.D., www.karpmandramatriangle.com) shines a light on our relationships. When we judge the conditions of others' lives, we invariably end up saying "I'm sorry" to those who join us in our dramatic interactions with one another. You can use the triangle below to picture how we often end up in places of regret, remorse, and unhappiness.

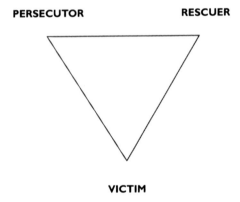

in our valued relationships with friends, family, and coworkers, we want our "sorries" to have lasting effects on our senses of self, status in groups, and overall well-being. In intimate relationships, we all tell our partners we're sorry once in a while.

The Karpman Drama Triangle is a very simple (yet enormously valuable) model I use to explain how many well-meaning people play the "sorry game" because they have weak boundaries and poor self-discipline. Few mature, well-functioning adults want to be thought of as Persecutors, but many of us end up playing this role. Persecutors are often seen as perpetrators by others in the triangle because, in their attempts to help, they offend Victims by getting in their way.

I've seen the Drama Triangle play out like this:

Bill has a friend named Sue who sees herself as a victim. She confides in Bill that her partner, Dennis, has become increasingly verbally abusive over time. Bill loves his friend and develops a dislike for Dennis, whom he sees as a bad person and wrong for Sue. Soon after Sue shares her upset, she and Dennis attend a party at Bill's home. When Dennis (whom Bill perceives as a Persecutor) says hello to Bill, Bill can't help himself and lets loose on the guy, telling him what a good-for-nothing lowlife he thinks Dennis is. As Dennis walks away, Bill thinks to himself, "Ah, that feels better."

Moments later, Sue confronts Bill in tears, saying, "How could you do that to me? You've betrayed my trust! I never want to see you again!" Then she and Dennis storm out of Bill's house. In that moment, all Bill can think to say is, "I'm sorry. I was only trying to help."

In this story, Bill fully engaged in the Drama Triangle. As a loving friend, he took on the role of Rescuer and stood up for Sue. When he confronted the alleged Persecutor, he stepped into the Persecutor role himself. When Sue reacted angrily to his actions, Bill got a taste of being a Victim and now sees Sue as his Persecutor.

Another scenario goes like this:

Ann has a co-worker named Donald. These two have functioned together in close quarters for some time and just don't connect.

One day, Ann sees Donald do something against company policy and shares this information with her supervisor. Much to her surprise, this supervisor calls Donald into her office, describes what she learned about him from Ann, and fires him on the spot. As soon as Donald relates these events to her colleagues, everyone in the office sees Ann as a snitch. They refuse to speak to her—or even look in her direction.

Ann initially saw herself as the company's Rescuer. She saw her company being victimized by Donald (the Persecutor). Although Ann and her supervisor believed Donald was wrong and deserved what he got, others in the office didn't see it that way. In their eyes, Ann was a Persecutor/Perpetrator. Hence they took on the role of Rescuers and defended their fired colleague. As a result, Ann now sees herself as the Victim of her peers' condemnation. All she can think to say to them is, "I'm sorry."

These are just two examples of how the Drama Triangle works. We enter the Drama Triangle and exchange roles in countless different ways. Once you enter this cycle, you're likely to experience all three positions—often more than once. Even worse, the Drama Triangle always leads you to the miserable role of Victim. There's no way to win this game—or end this dysfunctional dance—unless you see it for what it is and step away.

Consider these brief analyses of the three positions of the Drama Triangle:

THE
PERSECUTOR MIND-SET

Although they may not be aware of these subtle motivations, Persecutors act out of repressed anger and judgment. They're often filled with righteous indignation and seek to unmask others' wrongdoing without considering their feelings and intentions. Stereotypically, Persecutors could be seen as "dysfunctional fathers" or "nagging mothers" because they seek to expose and correct problems by directly attacking those they perceive as perpetrators. Persecutors consider intimidation from a sense of supremacy a perfectly acceptable method of justifying their perceived rightness.

Persecutors use blame to transfer their emotional (or physical) pain to others. What Persecutors fear most is being exposed as wrong or powerless. Although unconscious of their internal motivations, they attack others to hide their own sense of inadequacy. They focus on those they see as wrong to avoid dealing with their own inner demons. Persecutors perceive themselves as Rescuers and have no interest in saying "I'm sorry" until all seems lost. By then, they've moved on to the Victim position in the Drama Triangle.

The Persecutor path is one of self-imprisonment. These people live in dungeons of false superiority that require them to attack others repeatedly in order to protect their secret senses of failure.

THE
VICTIM MIND-SET

Victims feel unlucky and burdened by life—as if they've gotten the short end of the stick or a bad break. They see themselves as innocent, vulnerable, and fragile—and deny their power to create lives that work. They indulge in ideas like, "I'm sorry, but I just can't." Victims see themselves as fundamentally defective, incompetent, and unfixable. Often, they lay their failures at the feet of their perceived Persecutors.

Victims' perception of self-weakness doesn't prevent them from complaining to others about the great difficulties they face. They turn a deaf ear to possible solutions to their problems by saying, "That would never work for me." They desperately want (and likely expect) to be taken care of and inevitably pick people who are experts at the Rescuer role for this job. They lament to these Rescuers (as often as possible) about how they've been "done wrong" by those they view as Persecutors. Victims are "sorry" for all the moves they make in life—and everything that happens to them.

THE
RESCUER MIND-SET

Just as Persecutors are typified by the dysfunctional father, Rescuers are embodied by the stereotypically dysfunctional mother. Although this stereotype has a feminine slant, needing to fix things is very much a male tendency. "Protect and Defend" is the Rescuer's mantra. These people focus on righting wrongs—regardless of whether the Victims of these wrongs actually want them fixed.

One such man was in a difficult situation. He was separated from his wife and had custody of his two children. The three of them, for financial reasons, were living in his retired mother's home. Grandma had generously offered to care for her grandchildren so her son could transition into a new life while keeping his job and looking for a new residence.

When his children came home from school, they had more energy than their grandmother was accustomed to handling (as kids often do). When her son returned home one evening, she described how challenging the day had been for her. Because she talked like a Victim, it was easy for him to fall into the trap of Rescuing his mother from his kids (who were acting like Perpetrators).

So, in perfect Drama Triangle form, he jumped all over his kids about behaving badly around their grandmother. When he was done, and his kids felt completely Victimized by their father, Grandmother said to her son, "That wasn't what I wanted. I was just sharing my thoughts with you. Now my grandkids think I'm going to turn them in every time they act too much like kids."

All he could say was, "I'm sorry."

Rescuers look for problems—any problems. Fixing things makes them feel validated and valued. Helping others with their problems makes Rescuers feel worthwhile. They rescue others to cover up their own senses of inadequacy. Rescuers always keep their radars on and scan for problems to solve. Of course, when they seek out problems, they're guaranteed to find them.

And when it doesn't work out in the end, what do they say?

That's right . . . "I'm sorry."

The positions of the Drama Triangle are alluring—no one is immune to their call. Over the years, we've learned to find our favorite entry points; however, once we're inside, we move back and forth between these three positions. The only things that change are the faces of the players and the circumstances—the roles remain the same.

Plastered all over your triangle are the ever-lingering ghosts of "I'm sorry! I'm so sorry!" The problem is, these words we utter *so sincerely* are all lies. They don't change our behavior but they fall from our lips again and again—every time we enter this triangle of drama and ultimate despair.

We say we're "sorry" to stop the pain we're feeling. But not even groveling or making promises on the lives of our loved ones is enough. Our "sorry" feelings remain (as does the pain) for much longer than we'd like to admit.

How can we avoid such sorry circumstances?

The only way I know to escape the triangle is to avoid it entirely. Resist the temptation to step into alluring, judgmental situations—even when you perceive someone or something as wrong or bad. Just say no to the Drama Triangle . . . don't get hooked. Mind your own business!

Whatever it takes, don't fall into judgment—no matter what others do. You can't win! Remember that loving someone isn't a good reason to interfere in the conditions of their life. It just doesn't help.

When you disagree with people, don't perceive them as wrong. They aren't wrong; they simply have different perspectives from you. If you could observe other people's life from the moment they were born—through childhood, adolescence, and into adulthood—you could explain every action they took, no matter how inappropriate. Everyone is entitled to the thoughts and feelings they choose. Feeling inadequate is never a justifiable reason to drag someone else down. Liberate yourself by not buying into others' drama. It's a surefire way to avoid going down the rabbit hole that results in being sorry.

Have you ever seen someone treating another person poorly in public—a parent belittling a child or a man denigrating a woman? Didn't you want to tell these people what a jerk they were? You probably didn't, for fear they'd turn their hostility on you. More likely, they'd just tell you to mind your own business—or not hear you at all. People can rarely receive criticism when they're criticizing someone else. And—whether you're dealing with adults or children—admonishment is seldom an effective resolution to aggressive action.

One day, when I was at the beach with my wife, a man sitting near us began speaking loudly to a woman who appeared to be his wife or partner. What he was saying wasn't important, but the way he spoke to her with great judgment and indignation bled out all over the beach. The woman, clearly emotionally wounded, eventually got up and went into the water.

I wanted to tell him he was a bully, and he shouldn't speak to any human being (or animal, for that matter) as he had to his companion. In my delusional reactive thinking, I expected him to reply, "Oh, you're so right! How terrible of me to speak to her that way. I'm so sorry. I'll go apologize to her right away!"

Yeah, right. I knew any kind of confrontation would likely cause him to increase his level of upset and direct it either at her or back at me. When he looked my way and our eyes met, I said, "How wonderful it must be to have such a beautiful woman in your life."

He smiled begrudgingly and said, "Yes, it is." When she returned from the water, they spoke briefly (and softly), quickly packed their things, and left the beach.

With my simple question, I offered this man a chance to reframe his experience. I didn't find fault and humiliate him; I reminded him of what was important in his life. Clearly, his relationship with the woman was more than casual. She was important to him; he'd simply forgotten this in the moment. In the midst of whatever he was struggling with, he'd lost his internal compass. I confirmed this positive perspective some months later when I saw them again at the beach; they were loving and gentle with each other throughout the entire day.

When you act inappropriately, return to a place of emotional and mental balance. Align your actions with whatever is most important in your life. You can't correct reactive thinking by being sorry. Contrition only temporarily hides your delusions until they build up enough internal pressure to explode all over your life again.

Being sorry only exacerbates the cycle of dysfunction—it never corrects it.

5

THE GENDER EFFECT

According to numerous research studies, the genders don't equally embody the Sorry Syndrome. Psychologists who study gender differences in apologizing behaviors report that women are more prone to being sorry than men.

Experts have developed a number of theories about why men apologize less often than women. Based on their initial research, they suggest that men's lower incidence of apologizing may come from an inability to admit they've done wrong. Perhaps admitting wrongdoing feels like giving up power and creates a sense of vulnerability. Though many men behave this way, I know plenty of women who seek the upper hand in their relationships.

Some researchers think men are simply less conscious, perceptive, and concerned about what is or isn't socially offensive than women. This idea presupposes women are more socially attuned than men, and perhaps even overly sensitive to social standards. As a result, they may apologize more readily and frequently for their perceived offenses than men.

Other experts say women apologize more often because they place a higher value on relationships. However, I believe no one should feel the need to apologize just to maintain a friendship. A friendship that requires you to demean yourself isn't much of a friendship.

This apparent gender disparity in apologizing behaviors may fit into a much larger and more complex matrix of gender demands and expectations. For many generations, men were seen as providers and defenders of the family unit; they needed to appear strong and reliable when making choices for their families.

Women, on the other hand, were assigned to nurturing roles and didn't need to project a constant aura of invincibility. The institution of marriage was designed to provide safety and survivability for women and children. In these patriarchal societies, men were in charge. They needed to appear right and correct—no matter what. Logically (in such a lifestyle model), they would never have had a reason to apologize.

After World War II, America changed. People in the First World transitioned the focus of their relationships from survival to a quest for meaning. Today's relationships are all about feeling fulfilled and meeting our desires. This is a major reason why divorce in the States is so much more prevalent now than in the 1940s.

However, men today are still often referred to as the stronger gender. Though on average men are larger, faster, and stronger than women, a second look reveals that women live longer. Many women endure the physical burden of childbirth—which gives them a significant claim on being the stronger gender.

In two studies on gender and apologies, ("Why Women Apologize More Than Men: Gender Differences in Thresholds for Perceiving Offensive Behavior," *Psychological Science*), researchers Karina Schumann and Michael Ross found their female research subjects apologized more frequently than their male counterparts. In one study (September 20, 2010) women were more likely than men to feel that certain mistakes required apologies, although the researchers found no gender difference in the proportion of offenses that prompted apologies. Perhaps men apologize less frequently than women because they have a different definition of what constitutes offensive behavior.

Are men generally less self-critical than women, or do they just share their self-deprecating thoughts less easily and openly?

Experts suggest men may be less aware and more indifferent to how their words and actions affect others.

In their other study (November 2010) Schumann and Ross asked their participants to evaluate imaginary and remembered offenses. These study subjects evaluated the severity of a variety of hypothetical scenarios: someone not carrying their weight on a group project, a person in a grumpy mood barking at others, and someone waking up their partner in the middle of the night before an important job interview. The female participants in this study rated all of these scenarios more severely than the males did. Perhaps it takes more to offend men than women.

Though women in the U.S. may be over-apologizers, people in some cultures (for example Canadians) do the same thing, regardless of gender. Really! If you have Canadian friends, notice how often they apologize. Being sorry is even more of a cultural norm in Canada than in the U.S.

I found an intriguing piece of anecdotal evidence about gender differences in the title of comedian Jim Belushi's 2006 book on manhood: *Real Men Don't Apologize* (New York: Hyperion, 2007). In the book, Belushi addresses what it means to be a "real man." Though he offers advice on a variety of topics (such as dating, marriage, and sex), his book title shares the notion that apologizing is a weakness and conveys the idea that men should never be sorry. Well, he's half right. Men *shouldn't* be sorry, but neither should women.

We shouldn't see women's greater tendency to say "I'm sorry" as an indictment of wrongdoing. If women are more apt to be apology generators, men are more likely to misinterpret social standards and have a steeper social learning curve than women. How many times have you seen a male movie character saying, "What? What'd I do?!!"

We're all still learning how to coexist with one another as we move through life in the twenty-first century. Hopefully, we'll eventually learn to take responsibility for our actions without being sorry—and without considering gender.

The bottom line is this: whether you over-apologize or take less than full responsibility for your actions, being sorry isn't an effective remedy. We can all benefit from living balanced and integral lives without judging ourselves or others.

The thirteenth-century Sufi poet Rumi offers these words: "Rise up nimbly and go on your strange journey to the ocean of meanings. The stream knows it can't stay on the mountain. Leave and don't look away from the sun as you go, in whose light you are sometimes crescent, sometimes full."

6

IF I BELIEVED IN SIN, THERE'D BE FOUR

(BLAME—SHAME—REGRET—FAILURE)

It's true—I don't believe in the concept of sin. Sin is, by definition, a willful or deliberate violation of a religious or moral principle. According to this definition of sin, Martin Luther (founder of the Lutheran Church) must have sinned in 1517 when he sent his Ninety-Five Theses (inquiries) to the leaders of the Catholic Church. Today, however, he's remembered as an icon of the Protestant Reformation. Apparently, sin is a subjective idea in the minds of those who seek to control and cast blame.

So, who determines what's a sin and what isn't?

Small groups of people use religious and moral principles to impose their ideas on others and tell them how to live their lives. They say, "Do this—don't do that." I don't think so.

It's best to review each specific religious and moral principle you learned from your original family and place of worship before making it part of your doctrine for life.

Did some deity send us a set of rules—such as the Ten Commandments?

The people who came up with these directives simply saw what wasn't working in their culture and told people to do the opposite. Saying that these directives came from God probably worked well at the time. But we can embrace a greater reality by developing our own internal codes and choosing which standards to apply to our lives.

I'm not suggesting our civilized society doesn't need a system of laws. The writers of these codes have identified the lowest common denominators of behavior and listed standard punishments for those who don't comply. We, as a species, need laws—until we learn how to regulate our actions and set boundaries without them. Clearly, we aren't there yet.

I believe in impeccability. To me this means that what I think, say, and do is all the same. Impeccability is personal to each of us; we use it to create transparent lives. Impeccable people say what they mean and mean what they say. They act on their words and actions according to their internal thoughts. Interestingly, one definition of impeccable is "incapable of sin."

No one can hurt you unless you let them. Yes, others can hurt your body—but you aren't your body. Others can take, damage, or destroy your possessions—but you aren't your possessions.

When negative events happen in your life, you're always complicit in them. You chose to have a relationship with that person, take a job with that company, and move through life the way you did.

Your choices lead you to things you like and things you don't. You're far too actively engaged in your own circumstances to ever lay anything solely at someone else's feet. If you'd made different choices, you would have experienced different outcomes.

THE FOUR SINS

We stifle ourselves to the point that we have trouble living productive lives in four distinct ways: blame, shame, regret, and failure. Each one relates directly to the Sorry Syndrome. Sin, a concept I don't normally use, is perhaps the best word I know for describing the uselessness and futility of these four actions. Here's a look at each and how it results in unintended outcomes.

BLAME

Blame is the sin of perceiving fault in others. When things don't work out the way we'd like, we assign blame by pointing at the wrong person. Many people feel better by identifying a problem as completely separate from themselves. Blamers want others to take the fall by admitting their wrongdoing and being very,

very sorry. They assign blame to avoid taking responsibility for the conditions of their lives.

For some, every undesirable condition or problem has to be someone else's fault. Consider these ludicrous statements:

- I'm not successful because my parents wouldn't pay for my college education.
- I didn't get that promotion because my boss doesn't like me.
- I can't go on the vacation of my dreams because my partner doesn't want to visit that destination.

No one else is living your life. If you want something—anything—to exist in your life, you must create that outcome. The people around you (family members, friends, business associates, etc.) are the witnesses and observers of your life. They aren't (and can never be) the writers, producers, and directors of *your* story.

My Native American teacher, Will Rockingbear, once shared a story of visiting a community in South America. His host was a wealthy man who casually suggested he could arrange for a young local woman to visit Rockingbear that evening. "I'm married, and I won't be spending time with any other women," Rockingbear explained.

"Why not?" the man replied. "No one will know."

"I will," said Rockingbear.

Had Rockingbear made a different choice, he couldn't have—in good conscience—blamed his host for any fallout from his decision. As a result, he gained a great story to share with his apprentices.

So, who's to blame?

If you're quick to find fault or failure in people and situations, ask yourself these questions instead:

- What did I contribute to this situation?
- How did I play a role in bringing this about?
- What's been happening inside me that resulted in this outcome?

You can always learn from your honest answers to these kinds of questions.

Notice I didn't encourage you to ask, "What did I do wrong?" "How did I mess up?" or "Where did I make a mistake?" These self-blaming and shaming questions don't serve you. All of your actions (and others' actions, too) are neutral until you and the others who experience them place your individual values on them. We apply meaning to events and determine the value (or lack thereof) they bring into our lives.

No matter who the other players are in your story, you're always the primary creator of your experience. That's a good thing! If you can admit you've made a mess and created an undesirable outcome, you can replace it with something more to your liking. The possibilities are infinite—Yay!

SHAME

Shame is simply the sin of being sorry. It happens when people find severe fault in their actions and themselves. Shame, the root experience of "I'm sorry," involves turning blame inward.

Shamers deny there's anything to learn from their mistakes. They engage in internal abuse by bludgeoning themselves emotionally. Shamers may not give themselves visible bruises but inevitably create vast internal scarring.

If you're ashamed of your past, you spend much of your time and energy trying to keep it a secret. It's like having a second job. Every time you think about the object of your shame, you're stealing from the part of yourself that wants a life filled with joy and success. Every time you share your shame with others, you're asking them to look down on you. You want people to mirror your perceptions of yourself as weak, pathetic, and incapable of rising above your circumstances—and asking to be seen as sorry.

How does shame help us learn and grow?

It doesn't. We simply do what we do. All of our actions have value in our lives—if we take the time to learn from them and adjust our behavior accordingly. Shame blocks our learning and prevents us from growing in consciousness. No one can create a better life through shame. It's a dead-end street leading nowhere.

REGRET

Regret is a denial of the intrinsic perfection of life. It serves only to demean, belittle, and destroy our understanding of the precious and beautiful nature of who we are and why we're here.

When we commit the sin of regret, we hold ourselves in the past. It's as though life stops and replays itself over and over again. In our minds, we repeatedly relive embarrassing moments, accidents, assaults, verdicts, low test scores, broken promises, and countless other experiences. This repetitive rehashing of what didn't work in the past magnifies our anguish and increases the intensity of our most horrific memories. By wishing that these events had never happened, we make them larger and more painful. What a waste of time and intelligence!

Everything that's ever happened in your life has brought you to this moment. For most people, right now is pretty good. Is that true for you?

If it isn't, you probably need to release some regret. You gain nothing from dragging the baggage of your perceived failures, losses, shortfalls, etc. into your present moment. The only things worth carrying with you are the lessons that help you live a clearer and more productive life.

Rather than regretting a choice you've made, make another choice. Rather than regretting an action that didn't meet your expectations, create a new action. Rather than regretting the time, energy, and money you've invested in something without getting the return you expected, let it go. Put your time, energy, and money into something new and wonderful.

Life talks to us through all the circumstances and situations we experience. By putting effort into things that keep us in the past, we only end up feeling sorry. What a waste of life! Instead, let's put our efforts into activities that bring us more fully into the delight of being alive. Let's do the things that call us to be who we've come to planet Earth to be. *This* is where joy resides.

FAILURE

What I know about the sin of failure is that it doesn't exist; we invent this perception in our minds. We're creative by nature, so everything we express into our lives becomes the manifestations we experience. When we experience what we've created, those creations meet, exceed, or fall short of our expectations. Our creations are intact; they are what we created. But, if they fall short of what we think we wanted, we call them failures and find fault in them. By association, we find fault in ourselves.

Nonetheless, we separate ourselves from our perceived failures. By attempting to avoid the emotional discomfort that comes with these perceptions, we lose the opportunity to learn from our actions.

I once heard a story about a young executive with a Fortune 500 company. He was responsible for developing a project in which his company had invested a million dollars. After a while, the company felt the project didn't meet its expectations and abandoned it.

Feeling like an abject failure, this young executive went into the company president's office to tender his resignation. The president listened to the young man's sad story about how his failed efforts had cost the company a million dollars and then looked at him, totally perplexed. "Are you crazy?" he asked. "You can't quit. We've just invested a million dollars in your education."

If I'm not willing to learn from events that didn't go my way, how can I ever hone my skills and discover the efficacies of life?

The truth is, you've never failed at anything. You have, however, created exactly what you meant to put into your creation. This includes every thought, fear, doubt, and uncertainty that moved through your mind during the creative process.

Regardless of what you create, you always gain an opportunity to learn more about yourself. How could that be a failure?

To avoid sorry situations in your life, you must release your need to wallow and indulge in these four deadly sins: blame, shame, regret, and failure.

7

THE POWER OF I AM

In this chapter, I reference several Judeo-Christian concepts —though from a different perspective than most people are accustomed to. So, if you hold traditional views from either of these faiths, please know my intention is only to establish some very pragmatic and usable life skills. On the other hand, you may not follow either of these religious traditions. If that's the case, I encourage you to read through this section feeling no pressure to embrace any religious perspectives. These traditions simply provide an effective way of presenting several new and valuable ideas that are relevant to our exploration of the Sorry Syndrome.

Theologians define prophecy as the foretelling of what's to come. From a mystical or religious perspective, people believe that prophets are the messengers of the gods and their prophecies are divinely inspired messages.

The Christian Bible is full of material written by and about prophets. These messengers include Isaiah, Samuel, Ezekiel, Malachi, Jeremiah, and John the Baptist. The Bible also mentions prophetesses like Sarah, Deborah, Miriam, Hannah (Samuel's mother), and Isaiah's wife (who was actually called "The Prophetess"). The Greeks and Romans called their prophets oracles or seers. The Prophet Muhammad founded the Islamic religion. All of these people were revered for their ability to predict future events.

The idea of prophets seems odd to me because everyone can foretell the future—we do it all the time. We use the power of the original name of Divine Presence, as revealed to Moses in the Old Testament. Have you heard the story of Moses and the Burning Bush in the Book of Exodus? Moses was out in the fields, tending his father-in-law's flocks when all of a sudden, he saw a bush completely engulfed in flame.

Then from this bush came the voice of Yahweh (the Hebrew word for the ineffable or inexpressible Name) calling out to Moses and giving him specific instructions about freeing his people from Egyptian oppression. Moses was overwhelmed by his experience and felt reluctant to take on this task for he lacked the confidence to lead his people. So Moses asked, "What should I say if the people ask me your name?"

The voice replied, "I am the eternal God whose name is 'I AM.' People *must* use this name from now on."

Think about this: the eternal God is called I AM. Say the name of God out loud right now—I AM. Say it again—I AM. Who is God? I AM. Who is God? Go ahead, say it . . . I AM! Wow!

It's not my purpose in this book for you to consider the idea of the Divine Presence dwelling in, through, and as you. What I do want you to know, however, is the great power of the phrase I am. Using this phrase is, by its very nature, prophetic. Whatever quality, identity, or state of being you say after this phrase is prophetically declared.

You don't even have to say "I am" out loud. Whatever goes on in your thoughts and internal beliefs is pure prophecy. Yes—*you* are the prophet, the oracle, the great seer of your life.

When you say, "I'm sorry," you're making a prophetic declaration that diminishes your self-awareness, your effectiveness, and your ability to create the life of your dreams. I can't overstate the importance of this matter. The words you think and the words you utter reflect your beliefs and understandings of yourself and the world.

If you want to build a life filled with meaning and purpose, don't waste your energy and intelligence on ideas like being sorry. Remove any and all distractions that diminish the vision you have for your life. Yours is a divinely inspired vision, and you can't afford to place potholes and roadblocks along your path!

If you're thinking, "But I don't have a vision," remember *you* are the prophet of your life. In this moment, I'll assist you by being your interpreter. If you say you don't have a vision for your life, you're prophesying it will be filled with obscurity, mediocrity —and maybe even misery. Not very comforting, is it? This is the destiny of all who are sorry—all who receive the divinely given gift of life and squander it on anything less than vibrant health, abundant living, and loving relationships.

It's important to know that God doesn't care. I don't know of any deity that insists that you live a life of health, wealth, love, and happiness. However, if you have a vision for your life that brings forth your talents and gifts in meaningful ways and if you commit to the revelation of that vision, all of heaven and earth will align with the perfect unfoldment of your plans.

Even if you have a vision, some things can get in your way. I call these the False Prophets.

FALSE PROPHET #1
IMPATIENCE (THE INNER WORK)

When we doubt ourselves and the direction we're charting in our lives, we're playing the sorry game. To succeed in life, we must maintain a consciousness of persistence and perseverance. Don't force anything to happen in your life. All outcomes will arrive at just the right times—and in just the right ways. Our work is to be certain we're on the course that leads to the outcomes we desire. There's nothing wrong with changing course; the point is to take charge of the direction of your life with certainty—and without apology.

Our work is to diligently monitor our every thought and do whatever it takes to become the vision we hold in our hearts and minds.

To paraphrase the Master Teacher Jesus, "Whoever keeps asking, receives; whoever keeps seeking, finds; whoever keeps knocking will have the door opened unto them."

FALSE PROPHET #2
GETTING DISTRACTED FROM
YOUR VISION

"I'm sorry" is a great distraction, and all distractions are dangerous to your vision. What are your distractions?

- I'm not good enough, smart enough, educated enough . . .
- I had a difficult childhood.
- My ex-spouse took all my stuff.
- Things just don't work out for me.

And so on and so on, ad nauseam . . .

When we embrace these kinds of thoughts, they become self-fulfilling prophecies. Is that what you want? I certainly don't!

Be mindful when you engage in media activities. If you mindlessly accept what you see on TV, hear on the radio, or read on the Internet and in newspapers, you'll absorb those ideas into your consciousness and manifest them into your experience. Then you'll have lots more to be sorry about.

FALSE PROPHET #3
THINKING LIFE
IS ABOUT GETTING STUFF

In his letter to the Galatians, Paul writes, "You cannot fool God, so don't make a fool of yourself. You will harvest what you plant. If you follow your selfish desires, you will harvest destruction; but, if you follow the Spirit, you will harvest contentment."

Contentment comes from giving, having, and living your vision. *If you think your life is about gaining possessions, you're missing the point of the human experience.* Our individual lives are about bringing to the world the gifts that only we can bring.

Coincidently, when we focus on fulfilling our visions, we get far more stuff than we ever could have gotten by focusing only on getting stuff.

FALSE PROPHET #4
OTHERS' NEEDS, DESIRES, AND AGENDAS

Some people think they're helping you by feeling sorry for you—others get a twisted pleasure out of seeing you struggle. Some people love to give you advice—even with no experience to back it up. What do we call these kinds of people? All too often, we call them friends.

Think about those you call friends. These people are a reflection of your inner thoughts. They are the prophecies of who you're destined to be. As you observe who they are and how they live their lives, ask yourself: Is this who you want to be in the world?

Prosperous people surround themselves with other prosperous people. Successful people surround themselves with other successful people. People who are consciously awake surround themselves with other awakened beings. If you associate with people who exemplify the qualities you want in your life, they'll constantly remind and empower you to act—and help you become the powerful presence you're destined to be.

So, what do the prophets around you look like? Remember, *you* are the great Prophet, the Seer, and the Oracle of your life! What vision are you bringing forth? What are you prophesying for yourself and your life? This is yours—and only yours—to do.

Starting today, fill your mind with more useful and affirming thoughts and you'll immediately create a better life for yourself. Your old, worn-out, useless thoughts won't stop all at once. However, with time, diligence, and clear intention, those thoughts (just like being sorry) will disappear completely from your mind and your reality.

8

LEARNING FROM THE
BIG BOOK

In the teachings of the Alcoholics Anonymous fellowship, we can find some helpful guidance to understand the value of going beyond being sorry. As we all know, addiction to and abuse of alcohol and other drugs often include myriad behaviors that damage virtually all relationships in a person's life.

To help their participants recover from lives of dysfunction and helplessness, AA leaders offer the Twelve Steps. With this program, people can reclaim and restructure their lives after years of abuse. Two steps, in particular, speak to an action known as making amends:

- Step Eight: "[We] made a list of all persons we have harmed and became willing to make amends to them all."

- Step Nine: "[We] made direct amends to such people wherever possible, except when to do so would injure them or others."

You may think people recovering from alcoholism and drug addiction should apologize to everyone they've harmed during their times of substance abuse. But The Big Book doesn't call for apologies; instead, it asks participants to make amends.

By definition, *amends* means reparations or compensation for losses, damages, insults, or injuries. It's synonymous with recompense, redress, and restitution.

Making amends isn't about saying, "I'm sorry." It's about changing the nature of damaged relationships. This process begins when someone takes total responsibility for his past inappropriate actions by saying out loud, "This is what I did," in the presence of each person he harmed. Then the one making amends does whatever is necessary to make things right.

According to the Hazelden Betty Ford Foundation, making amends is about restoring justice. ("Making Amends Is More Than an Apology," John MacDougall, D. Min., July 23, 2015, www.hazelden bettyford.org/articles/macdougall/making-amends-is-more-than-an-apology). Imagine I borrowed $20 from a friend and never paid it back. Later, I went to that friend and said, "I'm sorry I borrowed that $20 and spent it on drugs." This apology changes nothing. However, what if I went to the person and said, "I borrowed $20 from you and used it to buy drugs. I'm clean now, and I'm managing my life much better. Here's your $20. I hope you can forgive me."

Making amends can include financial reparations and a variety of other actions, all of which are meant to demonstrate a change of heart and a sincere attempt to make things right.

The Big Book of Alcoholics Anonymous says, "Although these reparations take innumerable forms, there are some general principles which we find guiding. Reminding ourselves that we have decided to go to any lengths to find a spiritual experience, we ask that we be given strength and direction to do the right thing, no matter what the personal consequences may be. We may lose our position or reputation or face jail, but we are willing. We have to be. We must not shrink at anything" (p. 79).

Living up to this standard of behavior requires great courage and perseverance, especially when a person has left sizable devastation in their wake. Making amends has two purposes: (1) healing relationships as much as possible with those who have been negatively impacted by one's past actions; and (2) freeing oneself from the burdens of guilt and blame. People have practiced this powerful and proven method for generations—but not because it takes away painful memories or hurt feelings. It works because it shows that the person making amends is learning from his past and is willing and able to live in a more honest and productive way.

In some cases, people harmed by recovering alcoholics regard these amends (no matter how sincere) with skepticism and doubt. When this happens, AA suggests that the people in recovery not argue or insist on making amends and instead just back off. Hopefully, as time passes, those who've been harmed may become more open to the recovering addicts' offers.

Action steps like behavior changes and new ways of being in the world make our amends real and valuable. We'd all like our errors to simply go away so we can take an unburdened breath. We want to begin our lives again without having to fear that the gremlins of our past will show up uninvited. This freedom is the intended outcome of making amends, but it becomes real only through diligent work.

According to the teachings of AA, "We needn't wallow in excessive remorse before those we have harmed, but amends at this level should always be forthright and generous" (Big Book, p. 86). This guidance is valuable. Suffering never creates better outcomes. Only well-applied learning can accomplish lasting change and the better lives we seek.

9

THE POTENCY OF FORGIVENESS

We human beings are all cursed with the extraordinary ability to instantly find fault in one another—with remarkable regularity. Some of us are better at this than others. Sometimes, we choose not to judge someone, forget what happened, and simply move on. On other occasions, we hold on to our judgments like badges of honor. We're unwilling to let offenders off the proverbial hook, thinking that by holding them in states of wrongness, we're somehow causing them to suffer. Perhaps they *do* suffer, but not because of anything we've done. They suffer the consequences of their *own* thoughts and actions—just like the rest of humanity.

When we find fault in ourselves, we certainly find fault in others. Faultfinding perpetuates judgment and holds us in a state of separation. It keeps our misconceptions of being right or wrong (or good or bad) alive and active in our minds. These, in turn, influence the choices we make as we move through life. When this happens, there's no room for learning or understanding; we stay in our judgments and continue to find fault in ourselves and others. Faultfinding is somehow embedded in our psyche; we're hardwired to judge those around us.

The logical remedy to this condition is, of course, the practice of forgiveness. The old adage, "To err is human, to forgive divine," places a high value on the practice of forgiving those around us who we think have erred. Some say forgiveness is the perfect solution to judgment. It's certainly a deeply effective tool for reorganizing our lives and releasing our sense of having been *wronged*. It relieves the discomfort that arises when we observe people treating each other unjustly.

The most honorable people among us practice forgiveness as a daily activity. The rest of us tend to forgive others at least some of the time. But forgiving doesn't prevent us from engaging in the ongoing process of finding new faults in each other.

Some consider forgiveness the quintessential spiritual practice because it maintains good relationships between people. Teachers who practice forgiveness ask us to forgive—not to free offenders from our judgment, but to free ourselves from the burden of carrying judgment, and all the negativity it entails.

Spiritual teachers identify many levels of blame. They ask us to peel them away (like onion layers) until there's nothing left to forgive. Forgiveness sets our souls free to rise, unencumbered. By forgiving everyone (including ourselves) for everything we've ever judged as less than perfect, we experience wondrous psychological benefits.

This all sounds well and good, but we must be careful not to misunderstand and misapply the practice of forgiveness. For example, when we say "I'm sorry," we typically think we're asking for forgiveness; however, we're also finding fault in ourselves. Similarly, when we expect or accept apologies from others, we acknowledge faults in them.

What can we do to escape this downward spiral of repeatedly blaming and forgiving each other?

We are, as many wise masters have taught, the creators of our experiences. Those around us are reflections of our consciousness; they are actors in our plays as we create the events of our lives through our thoughts.

The glitch for me is that my awareness remains fully engaged during the act of forgiveness. As I forgive someone on a conscious level, I simultaneously find fault in him (and myself) on other levels. Remember, if you have something to forgive, you must first have found fault in someone's actions.

As I've said many times in this book, we should never be indifferent to the results of our actions. I believe in taking complete responsibility for everything I do. Life is so much easier when we

1. Realize we're creating the circumstances of our lives.

2. Seek to understand why things don't turn out the way we planned (i.e., someone gets upset with us).

3. Devote time and attention to learning what we can from our negative experiences, so we don't have to experience them again and again.

When we feel especially injured by others' actions, we withhold forgiveness. We say, "They don't deserve my forgiveness." We think this withholding will somehow get us something to compensate for our immense suffering. What we're actually doing, however, is holding ourselves in states of judgment. We waste our energy and attention by being upset and guarded while trying to protect ourselves from people we perceive as awful.

I'm far too lazy to spend my energy this way with anyone for very long. Instead, I learn the same way I do when I've offended someone. I know from a lifetime of observation that people tend to be true to their natures. If someone lies to me, it's highly likely they'll lie to me again. I shouldn't hate them, judge them, or see them as less than whole. Instead, I can simply trust them to be true to their nature.

Trusting people to stick to their nature isn't an absolute rule. Just like you and me, everyone is constantly learning and changing at their own pace and in their own way. Still, *we* shouldn't expect them to change into what we want them to be.

We can expect people to habitually act out (what we perceive as) their character flaws. If, however, they choose to change their ways, we can celebrate those changes with delight. If we assume they'll keep behaving as they do, we can be delightfully surprised when they choose a different attitude or action. When this happens, tell them, "Yay! Good for you!" Then, wish them well and move on.

By adopting the above approach, you'll only be surprised when things get better. People who don't change should never surprise us. That's just who they are—and that's the way they participate in life.

People who say, "I'm sorry," tend to stay true to their natures by not learning from their actions. They aren't bad people; however, we know what to expect from them, which can be helpful in our ongoing interactions.

I've made it my personal practice not to accept people's apologies. Store clerks, food servers, ticket agents, and others that work with the public are quick to be sorry when products don't work and services aren't delivered as expected. Customer service representatives are trained to apologize whenever their customers are inconvenienced or annoyed. Phone systems even have recorded messages that say, "I'm sorry, but this isn't a correct number."

Instead of saying, "Oh, no problem," or "Don't worry about it," I say, "You have nothing to be sorry about." Then, I engage them in conversations about how I can get what I want. It's highly unlikely the person saying they're sorry built the product that doesn't work or cooked the meal incorrectly. Their apologies just don't fit; there's nothing to forgive, only something to resolve.

Resolution is always the most important task; being sorry is no help at all. Let's figure out how to create outcomes that are in the best interest of everyone involved.

PART II

MOVING BEYOND

10

PERSONALITIES AND PREFERENCES

So, if we aren't going to say "I'm sorry" anymore, what can we do? How can we navigate those moments when we participate in events that don't turn out the way we want?

Sometimes, we damage or lose things. Sometimes, we emotionally and physically injure people. Other peoples' sensibilities won't always align with ours. Just because we've chosen to act differently in the world doesn't mean others will automatically accept or embrace this change.

How can we establish a new level of conscious awareness that results in a more effective way of being in the world?

For the Sorry Syndrome (or any other obsolete social standard) to shift, our entire culture needs to adopt a new communication style. This transition will surely take many years.

So, how can we participate in and facilitate this shift?

This enormous change starts with *us*. We must commit to letting go of apologizing and consciously choose higher actions.

After a lifetime of being sorry on a regular basis, how can we avoid slipping back into this habitual and culturally encouraged behavior?

I have some ideas about how to accomplish this, and I'll certainly share them with you. But, before I do, I want to offer you the opportunity to unravel this mystery for yourself. We need to develop many alternatives to saying "sorry" because this habit is so enticing. Surely, different strategies will resonate with different people.

People don't process information in the same ways. Personality psychology experts examine the similarities and differences in our behaviors. This exploration formally began with Gordon Allport's work in the late 1930s. Since then, many researchers (including Swiss analytical psychologist Carl Jung) have sought to explain and demonstrate the functions of our various emotional temperaments. Katharine Briggs and Isabel Myers (a mother-daughter team) extrapolated Jung's ideas into their famous personality test, the Myers-Briggs Type Indicator.

Experts in this extensive field of study often align the four main personality types with four primary mythological archetypes. Through exhaustive experimentation, they've shown that people typically choose one of these four archetypes over the other three.

Robert Moore and Douglas Gillette encourage people to explore and consider the qualities of each archetype to identify their primary archetype (*King, Warrior, Magician, Lover: Rediscovering the Archetypes of the Mature Masculine.* San Francisco:

Harper, 1990). However, even though you may have a favorite archetype, you'll still resonate somewhat with the others.

Below, you'll see four attribute lists that describe the four archetypes. Read through these brief descriptions and determine which feels the most familiar. They all contain desirable traits, but you'll feel a stronger match with one than the other three. Read this as many times as it takes for you to feel a connection. Let the essence of each list wash over you, and soon you'll know which one best describes you.

CHOOSE A GROUP
(A, B, C, OR D)

A · Relationships, connections, and harmony are highly important to you.

· You have lots of friends—both human and furry.

· You pride yourself on being authentic and unique.

· You can often sense what other people are feeling.

· People are far more important than things.

· You enjoy aesthetics, music, and nature.

· You're a caring, empathetic listener.

· You thrive on recognition and acceptance.

· You excel at motivating people.

B · Discovering, learning, and understanding are of primary importance to you.

· You love solving problems, finding solutions, and experiencing new things.

- You like to be correct and accurate.
- You admire intelligence, competence, wit, and wisdom in others.
- You're curious by nature and enjoy exploring abstract ideas.
- You must be proficient at whatever you do.
- Unlocking the secrets of the universe excites you.
- You know that knowledge has power.

C
- You're always up for a challenge.
- You enjoy exploring new frontiers.
- Life is an incredible adventure.
- You revere bravery and courage in others.
- You're loyal to the ideals you hold sacred.
- You passionately defend your beliefs.
- Honesty and integrity are your primary virtues.
- You're willing to take on tasks that scare other people.
- You know how to be a reliable friend, employee, and team player.

D
- You value tradition, authority, and responsibility.
- You like helping people make good choices.
- You're well-organized, productive, and a top contributor.
- You anticipate and prepare for the future.
- Success and excellence are essential qualities in your life.
- You appreciate awards and public recognition.
- You work well within structures, laws, and boundaries.

CHAPTER 10

WHICH ONE ARE YOU?

☐ A

☐ B

☐ C

☐ D

IF YOU AREN'T SURE,
READ THROUGH THEM AGAIN.

These archetypes, as I explained earlier, all have names. I withheld them until now so they wouldn't influence your choice.

TABLE OF ARCHETYPES	
A	LOVER
B	MAGICIAN
C	WARRIOR
D	KING/QUEEN

Now that you've identified your archetype, reread its list of traits one more time. Isn't it uncanny how they describe your way of being in the world?

Using this new information, consider how you'd respond to the following three scenarios (without apologizing):

1. You're distracted from driving for a moment—just as traffic slows down. You bump into the car in front of you. You and the other driver pull off the road and get out to assess the situation. You can see you've dented his bumper. What do you say to this person?

2. Your two best friends invite you on a special weekend trip to do something you all love. You tell them you'll cover a third of the expenses if they make all the arrangements, which they do. A few days before your trip, a valuable business opportunity arises that conflicts with your weekend plans. You value this opportunity, so you say Yes! What do you tell your friends?

3. Someone shares a personal story and asks you not to tell anyone. You agree. Days later, in conversation with someone else, you unthinkingly repeat the information you promised to keep private. You didn't consciously intend to break your friend's confidence; you just weren't paying attention. How do you resolve this issue?

I've conducted this exercise with groups at conferences and workshops across the United States. I've observed a degree of alignment between people's "sorry strategies" and their primary archetypes.

ARCHETYPAL SORRY STRATEGIES

LOVERS typically focused on the other person (or people). Were they all right? What did they need? Lovers were primarily interested in helping and supporting those they had hurt. How could they make it up to their friends for missing the weekend? How could they regain their friend's trust? They sincerely wanted to make everything okay again.

MAGICIANS focused on the details of the experience. They cared about others but quickly turned their attention to the information they could ascertain or provide to rectify these situations. In the accident scenario, they wanted to know if the other person's taillights were fully functional. They sought to understand why they were driving distracted. Magicians looked for quick ways to rectify these problems. In the case of the trip with friends, they were very willing to admit their business opportunity was more important than a vacation. In the broken confidence example, they wanted their friend to see their behavior as an isolated incident.

WARRIORS primarily focused on fixing the problem in each scenario. They were flexible about the means but unyielding in seeking workable solutions to these issues. They wanted to repair the car, reschedule the trip, and reestablish trust with their friends. Quick, complete, and absolute resolutions were tantamount to any other considerations. They *knew* they could make everything all right.

KINGS/QUEENS (also called Sovereigns) took a broader view of these circumstances than the others. They tended to be good negotiators with clear perceptions of what they wanted. They liked having things work out for everyone but demonstrated strong feelings about how that should look. They were unaffected by others' emotional reactions and unattached to others' rate of progress to full resolution. It might seem like they didn't care about the other people in the scenarios; but, more accurately, they were just less likely to get emotionally hooked. In each situation, they were confident that moving beyond the problem was mostly a matter of choice and knew that the details would work themselves out.

Do any of these approaches resonate with you? None of them are right or wrong; however, they're much more valuable than simply being "sorry." These are all legitimate methods of resolving the unintended results of our actions. Even without apologies, these resolutions feel sincere and uncompromised.

So far, you've developed a personal strategy for taking genuine responsibility for your actions and avoiding the perils of being sorry. Now, let's look at the other side of the coin. What happens when someone acts inappropriately toward *you*—and then says nothing? Doesn't that just set you off?

Most of us get hooked into thoughts like, "This isn't fair" and "What they did was wrong" when we want apologies and don't get them. We might think, "They owe me an apology, and I want it now!" To move beyond apologies, we must change this part of our mental wiring.

When we want an apology, we're asking for next to nothing. Apologies are hollow; expecting them wastes our time and energy. We may think we want people to be sorry; however, we really want people to justify their offensive or inappropriate actions.

Years ago, researchers conducted a study on an unsuspecting group of people waiting in line for a service. A stranger walked up to them and asked to cut in line, using one of two approaches:

"Can I get in line ahead of you?" and "Can I get in line ahead of you because . . .?"

When the stranger used the first approach, they were seldom allowed to cut in. People almost always told them to go to the end of the line. The second approach, however, worked most of the time. Amazingly, it didn't seem to matter what followed the word "because." It was only necessary for the person making the request to justify cutting in line.

Being sorry can function the same way.

Some people say, "I'm sorry . . . it'll never happen again." How do you feel when you hear this?

Most people would gladly accept this promise, believing it sincere. They'd feel able to maintain trust with this person after a crisis.

Our culture doesn't demand these promises from us; we offer them freely. For this reason, I suggest a new, more meaningful way of dealing with these interpersonal interactions that can create higher levels of integrity.

My approach has four elements:

1. I admit what I did.
2. I describe my perception of what happened (without defending myself).
3. I share what I've learned.
4. I state my new intention.

In the next chapters, I'll weave these concepts into a formula for practicing authentic responsibility. Soon, you'll never again utter the words, "I'm sorry."

11

TAKING
AUTHENTIC RESPONSIBILITY

STEP ONE:
THIS IS WHAT I DID

We human beings, by nature, live in a constant state of habitual and repetitive activity; we do things over and over again, every day. Most of us wake up at the same time each day. We go through many routines: drinking the same beverages, administering regular hygiene and grooming activities, dressing in our usual attire, driving along the same roads, speaking as we usually do, and so on.

We undertake most of these daily habits without thinking consciously about them; we just do the same things every day. We believe these habits are the best ways to move through our lives.

However, our belief systems differ, just like our DNA codes. We share most of our 20,000 to 25,000 genes with all other humans, but no one is exactly the same except identical twins, whose bodies came from the same developing embryo. However, even twins have individual personalities and belief systems.

Our genes determine the color and texture of our hair, the shape of our faces, our height, our genders, and a vast number of other physical characteristics. Our belief systems determine our consciousness and the way we interact with our environment. Just as much of our DNA is the same, we humans also share many beliefs; experts call this "race consciousness."

We believe the world is round; we believe the sun will rise in the morning and set in the evening. We also share many beliefs about how life works. However, in our personal lives, we form unique impressions of and perspectives on life—which influence our belief systems.

Unlike DNA, our belief systems develop and change throughout our lives. We can add to or subtract from these systems by changing our minds about particular beliefs. We establish most of our beliefs when we're very young and impressionable—and then spend the rest of our lives justifying these beliefs. We aren't stuck with our beliefs, however. We're all at choice; we can change our beliefs in an instant. The point is, although more than seven billion people live on this planet, we're all unique individuals. We each have our own concepts of what's real and what isn't.

As we interact with one another, we learn that some of our beliefs align with those of our peers; however, some of our beliefs differ widely from the norm. These differences can cause us to collide with each other in varying states of disagreement and judgment. We have strong opinions about what works and what doesn't work. We know what we like and what we don't. Most of us (especially extroverts) are quick to share our preferences with others. We operate from the premise that we clearly understand how life works for us—and everyone else. When we operate from the premise of a single reality, we assume everyone sees and experiences life as we do. This perception of reality creates conflict in our lives.

The memories of our experiences are the foundations of our realities. When other people challenge our realities with their speech or behavior, we often automatically disagree with or judge them. We aren't consciously aware of it, but this is the exact opposite of communication—especially if we tell them they're wrong and we're right. Only with clear and honest communication can we bridge the chasm between what we believe and what others have experienced.

Communication isn't about convincing others to agree with us. But we sometimes hold such strong beliefs that we're compelled to try. Our beliefs are important to us (and they should be). We use them to organize our lives, feel safe and in control, and maintain our realities. This is a good thing.

If I asked you to make a list of all your beliefs, you couldn't do it. Our brains don't organize our mental functions as lists. Throughout our lives, we've all developed thousands of beliefs. We often become aware of them only when related events stimulate our brains to access them. However, this doesn't mean our beliefs are inactive until we need them. Our beliefs are all fully active in our subconscious minds, ready to pop into our conscious awareness at any moment. They typically show up as reactions to particular stimuli. When this happens (and it happens all the time), we usually consider our beliefs absolutely true and accurate —and defend them vigorously.

If I asked about your beliefs regarding abortion, you could surely tell me in great detail what you believe and why you believe it. When you watch or read news reports about events at abortion clinics, you react instinctively, according to your beliefs about abortion. When this happens, you don't learn anything. Instead, your subconscious mind uses these experiences to reinforce your existing beliefs.

In 2008, the federal government bailed out the mega insurance company AIG with billions of dollars. When certain company executives took bonuses from this bailout money, there was a massive public outcry. Many people wanted the government to prosecute and imprison these executives. Members of Congress threatened to tax these bonuses at 90 percent.

Amid this upset, one AIG executive wrote a letter to his company's chief executive officer. The *New York Times* subsequently published this letter in its editorial section (www.nytimes.com/2009/03/25/opinion/25desantis.html). In this missive, the executive explained that his employment contract called for him to receive one dollar in annual compensation and a performance-based bonus at the end of his contract period. He pointed out that the division of AIG he managed was substantially profitable. He and his team worked long hours day after day—and met every objective their bosses assigned. They deserved the compensation they had earned, according to their employment contracts.

I, like most people, was quietly critical of the entire AIG mess. I felt it was appropriate for managers who took bonuses to endure crowds protesting in front of their homes. I felt they deserved the pressure several state attorneys general were putting on them to return this money. But, when I read this article, I realized I couldn't judge the actions of this large and diverse group of people; they weren't equally culpable for their company's plight. To create fair outcomes for all, authorities must consider each person's individual punishment or reward.

The day after I read this article, I shared this experience with a friend at a social gathering. Others overheard me, joined the conversation, and challenged my stance. One woman took great exception to what I said. She said my perspective didn't matter and insisted all AIG executives were crooks!

For me, this letter had been an eye-opener. However, this woman wouldn't consider any possibilities beyond her beliefs. She showed me how we often cling to our beliefs, especially when we invest our emotions in them. When we're unwilling to alter our beliefs, we don't learn; when we don't learn, we become less resilient. The resulting state of stagnation only perpetuates itself.

So, how does all this apply to taking authentic responsibility?

To be authentically responsible, we must be "able to respond." That's what the word responsible means. To be responsible, we must be willing to learn. We must be willing to learn from our experiences and offer this opportunity to those around us. When someone finds fault with us, we must create an open channel of communication. We have likely precipitated a communication disconnect with our actions; we must address this breach before creating understanding with the other person. Our first order of business is to reestablish this connection.

Being sorry doesn't open lines of communication; in fact, it decreases communication. Only open and two-way verbal and emotional interactions create communication.

By beginning a conversation with, "This is what I did," you create agreement on the event in question—the first step in creating a learning experience. What you believe happened and what the other person believes may differ widely. You won't know until you start communicating with one another.

When I practice this step in my life, I'm amazed by the differences between my experiences and those of others. I might be certain that a person is overreacting and being unreasonable. But when I explain what happened on my end (without making the other wrong or diminishing his perspective), I open a door for us to share how we experienced the same event.

For example, I might say, "Wow, I didn't know this was so important to you. What I said was that by going back to school and getting your degree, you'd surely feel better about yourself. That was a presumptive thing for me to say, but I had no idea you'd react the way you did. What's your take on what happened?"

At this point, I stop talking and listen intently.

If the other person responds reactively, that's okay; he may have hurt feelings. This experience may have triggered his internal beliefs of not being good enough without a college degree, previous unpleasant college experiences, and many others. The purpose here isn't to instantly align your perspective with the other person's. Instead, just explore what happened.

What happened includes more than what you said or did. These events were just the beginning of a series of reactions (which can all occur in an instant). Every experience elicits an internal or external reaction; every reaction elicits a counter-reaction. In our culture, the default counter-reaction is to be sorry. However, when we're sorry, we don't learn anything; if we don't learn anything, nothing changes.

We can reestablish communication with others by agreeing on what initiated the issue at hand. Throughout this process, we increase our awareness of each other.

When we communicate our perceptions of our experiences with others, we invite them to respond in kind. If they choose to share with us (and we choose to listen intently), we may well learn something about them—and ourselves. This knowledge is our reward for taking the time to communicate.

This approach even applies to small events like bumping into someone in the hallway, spilling something on a person, and other small missteps. Taking time for an instant recap puts everyone on the same page. By saying you did what you did, you create a potential for understanding. This first step can help you begin aligning your ideas with those around you.

Remember, this beginning step doesn't resolve anything. Rather, it opens up lines of communication so everyone involved in a situation can start moving toward agreement and connection.

STEP TWO:
THIS IS WHAT HAPPENED

Using a multiple-step process to address issues with others may not feel natural to you. But, once you see how it all fits together, you'll be amazed by how quickly you can resolve conflicts with this method. For now, just be patient and give this process a chance.

In Step One, you got the attention of a person who felt wronged by you. You stated you'd done something that didn't turn out well. By doing so, you laid a foundation for further communication. You also found a common point of agreement; the other person said, "Yes, that's what you did."

Now that both of you are on the same page, you need to agree on what resulted from your initial action.

Step One wasn't about explaining why you did what you did; the other person wasn't interested in your excuses. Instead, you did your best to understand, acknowledge, and take responsibility for your actions. Accepting your less-than-desirable behaviors isn't easy, but it's essential for achieving valuable outcomes.

Looking back on a conflict, you can't know everything that happened. How could you possibly know what the other person was thinking? You might be very aware of his emotional state, but you don't know what caused it—until he shares his thoughts.

PROCESSING UNRESOLVED EMOTIONS

When we stay upset about something for more than twelve seconds, we aren't upset about the matter at hand; we're experiencing unresolved issues anchored in our memories. An event has triggered an unresolved (and likely unconscious) trauma in our psyche.

When others react to your behavior with more intensity than your original action, you've stimulated a similar memory in them—which probably has nothing to do with you. You just happened to push one of their internal buttons and hence received the brunt of their auto-response to a reoccurring and unresolved issue. Ouch!

At some time or another, we've all erupted emotionally due to our unresolved issues. If you want to clean up your subconscious clutter, try this easy method:

- Get out several sheets of unlined paper.

- Sit in a quiet place where you won't be disturbed (give yourself at least two hours).

- Write down the name of each person (or as many as you can remember) toward whom you've ever felt anger, resentment, fear, embarrassment, or any other emotional distress.

The first name on your list will likely be your mother. Begin by writing down the name you first called her (Mom, Mama, Mommy, etc.). As you do, conjure up the memory of an experience when you felt hurt by her. Don't tell yourself you can't remember any pain. Even in the healthiest relationships, people say and do things that hurt each other. Your feelings are there; when you remember and feel one, all you have to do is consciously let it go. *Realize it isn't happening now.* It happened a long time ago; there's no reason to hold onto it anymore. Let it go!

When the emotion and memory you've attached to this parent fades, you probably feel centered again. Now, write down the name you first called your father and go through the same process of conjuring up a hurtful memory and letting it go. Do the same for each of your siblings, all your childhood friends, and any neighborhood kids you can remember. Then, do your teachers, grade-by-grade, and anyone else you can remember from your grade school and college days. One person at a time, remove the unresolved emotional sludge from your past.

Once you've processed your spouses, bosses, coworkers, and everyone else you can think of (including your mentors and spiritual teachers), destroy this very long list. You can burn it, bury it, flush it, or just throw it in the garbage—just get *rid* of it.

Then, when you're ready, get out several more sheets of unlined paper and go through the process again. Sit in a quiet place where you won't be disturbed and write down the name of every person with whom you had a conflict, starting with your mother or father. You'll likely observe that the second round of this process is quite different from the first. Feelings about certain people will be different, possibly even neutral, whereas strong emotions arose during the first round. If you're visual by nature, different images may come to mind, as you move from person to person.

You may be amazed by how clear and aware you become after repeating this simple process a number of times.

WHAT HAPPENS DURING THIS PROCESS

All your life, you've experienced others through relationships. While many relationships provide us with cherished memories, they can also hold hurtful ones. When we don't resolve these painful experiences, we have to spend some of our focus on continually pressing these unresolved emotions down into our subconscious mind—where they fester over time.

As my first spiritual teacher explained, we all have a finite ability to pay attention to the activities and occurrences of our lives. Let's say we each have 1,000 units of attention with which to focus on the activities of our lives. When all 1,000 units are available, we can use them to focus any activity we choose. If we could do that all the time, we'd be a bunch of geniuses! But every time something happens that upsets us, we have an emotional reaction. Sometimes, we can work out our upset so this experience quickly becomes neutral and unimportant to us; however, that isn't what usually happens.

Most events in our lives that trigger our emotions remain unresolved because instead of neutralizing them, we bury them unresolved in our subconscious mind. We hold them there with the necessary number of attention units to keep them from our conscious awareness. However, similar (but unrelated) experiences can inadvertently create emotional responses in us—though we don't know why.

Here's an example. A father observes his son doing something inappropriate and tells him he's stupid. This hurts the son deeply, but the boy doesn't know what to do with all the pain. So instead of confronting his father, he buries the experience deep within his subconscious and forgets about it. But it's still there, which means that whenever anyone suggests he's stupid—or that he isn't bright, smart, or capable—he flares with great anger and upset in a way he doesn't understand. Others don't understand him either; they just think he has a bad temper.

As we go through life, we use some of our 1,000 attention units to keep our unhealed feelings at bay. The more this happens, the fewer attention units we have available to focus on what's happening in our current experience, and our ability to effectively pay attention becomes less and less functional. As a result, we seem less present and far less able to deal with what's going on in our lives.

By releasing the pressure of these unresolved memories and emotions, we can reclaim our precious attention units. We can apply more and more of these 1,000 units to our daily activities, thereby increasing our perceived intelligence and connection to the present moment.

When I first did this process of releasing, my second round revealed memories of several people who hadn't been on the first list. I cleared unresolved conflicts with many individuals as I wrote their names on my initial list. As I released my upset with them, many of these names didn't come up in my second round. In their place, other memories surfaced. As I found and cleared many of these unresolved memories, the list continued to change. In rounds three and four (yes, keep doing this again and again) the list shrank considerably. As a result, I became more and more present to my current reality. I was actually getting smarter!

Give this process a try and watch for improvements in your thoughts and attention span. Soon after I returned from Australia (where I learned this technique for cleaning up my mental faculties), I was watching the television game show *Jeopardy*. On that particular night, with absolutely no effort, I spoke each question correctly out loud before the contestants could even reply. It seemed quite surreal as it was happening. I attribute my ability in that moment to my much-improved capacity to pay attention.

PROCESSING OTHERS' EMOTIONS

The deep and lengthy process I've just described can help us be more present in the moment; however, it's of little value to those around us, especially when we've done something that causes them distress. Fender benders, using our outside voice indoors, getting in others' way, and similar momentary offenses may lead to drama with others who just can't deal with them. In these moments of seeming crisis, we may have to endure some trash talk (if the other person chooses to go that route). In this case, remember you're experiencing the results of your initiating action; listen beyond the other person's emotional eruption and try to understand what's going on inside him.

When confronted by these emotional onslaughts, most people say they're sorry to avoid conflict. However, you must take control of your emotional state; don't get hooked into emotional battles that have no winners. Hear the other person out.

You can even facilitate this exchange. As my colleague, Dr. Gary Simmons, suggested in his book *The I of the Storm,* try saying, "Tell me more."

By inviting others to share their words and feelings, you can stand in your clarity and receive whatever they have to say. You can glean useful information from their communication—if you can transcend your discomfort and really *hear* them. Trust the process; resolution can come only when both parties clearly exchange their ideas. Demonstrating the patience to guide the other person into this kind of interaction shows your emotional maturity and psychological power.

When an undesirable event occurs and you don't say "I'm sorry," remember the other person understands his experiences better than anyone. He probably won't be open to hearing your perceptions until he feels you've fully heard and understood him.

ENGAGING WITH SOMEONE WHO ISN'T COMMUNICATING

Some people may shut down and emotionally withdraw. They may display body language cues like crossing their arms or looking away. These people just aren't going to say anything right now. If this happens, take charge and encourage the flow of communication toward resolution.

STEP ONE:

"This is what I did." Take responsibility up front. Let them know you're paying attention.

STEP TWO:

"This is what happened as a result." Offer your perspective on what happened as clearly and succinctly as possible without defending yourself.

Then, ask, "Is that what happened?" which lets the other person think about the situation and take a position. Next, he'll either agree with you or provide more information to expand on what you said. This communication moves the two of you closer to resolution.

For this process to work, you must sincerely listen and give the other person your full attention; you have much to gain from this information exchange. Begin to learn what you can from what happened—the next step in this process.

STEP THREE:
THIS IS WHAT I'M LEARNING

In the first two steps, you took an action, admitted what you did, observed the results of your action, and stated out loud how it affected the others in the situation. You asked them if they agreed with your perspective—or if there was more to know.

Now that you've listened to those affected by your action, it's time to figure out what you've learned from this experience—and say it out loud. Everyone with whom we interact is in our lives to reflect back to us who we are and why we're here on planet Earth. Through these people, we can observe and learn from the results of our actions.

What you say next in this situation is essential to resolving it in a meaningful way. Learn whatever you can from this experience—so you don't have to go through it again.

Step Three bears many similarities to the "making amends" segments of Twelve Step programs (see Chapter 8, Learning from the Big Book). When you amend something, you change it for the better. You change your understanding, which leads to a behavior change. These "amendments" improve your relationships with others (and your life, in general).

It helps to say you didn't intend to hurt, upset, disrespect, or otherwise offend the other person—if and only if this is true. If you acted in anger or spite, it's okay (and even helpful) to admit it—so long you as aren't making excuses to validate your behavior. We're more prone to create undesirable outcomes when we're upset; recognizing this in yourself can motivate you to change your behavior.

It's okay to say you feel bad about what's happened, but don't dwell there. Remorse, regret, and guilt won't help you take responsibility for who you are in the world. Contrition, by itself, won't change your behavior.

Focus on consciously understanding what you're learning from the experience at hand. Being clear and open makes a great difference with people. Everyone makes mistakes, but most people aren't willing to take authentic responsibility and modify their behavior to avoid repeating their missteps.

Always set a personal intention of learning from your mistakes by walking through the fire of that learning. Admitting that what you did wasn't helpful (or was even harmful) can be hard on your ego. Fessing up can leave you vulnerable and unsure of yourself unless you clearly intend to clean up something that didn't work. Learn from this experience, so you don't have to go through it (or a similar one) again.

It's important to say what you've learned out loud and identify the resulting intentions you've set. You primarily benefit from your mistakes via this learning and growth. When you learn what doesn't work and adjust your behavior, you probably won't repeat your negative experiences. The people around you may see that even though you've made missteps in the past, they don't have to worry about your repeating the same (or similar) errors.

What you do is always more important than what you say. However, you do need to state your intentions out loud for others to hear. Of course, you should articulate your statements of intention with words that feel right in the moment. I've provided some examples to get you started:

- "What I did and how it affected you makes me see that making hurtful statements to you or anyone else just doesn't work."
- "Thank you for helping me see and understand that what I say really does matter."
- Having gone through this helps me remember I love you."
- "Being disrespectful like this is incongruent with who I am. I do respect you."
- "I get that I have to slow down and pay attention to where I'm going."
- "I don't want this thing I did to get in the way of our friendship/ relationship. You're more important to me than that."
- "I'm working on forgiving myself. I hope you can you forgive me, too."
- "I'm clear that withholding information from you never helps."
- "Doing that was shortsighted. I can do better."
- "You're more important than this thing I was defending. Going through this experience helped me remember that."

- "I was being selfish. I now realize I get more from life when I'm generous."
- "When I allow myself to be distracted, things go poorly."
- "I've realized that being stubborn makes my life a lot harder."
- "Taking out my frustrations on you never helps."

You can create thousands of other statements of learning. Whatever you choose to say, *be sincere*. This statement is primarily for *you*—you're the one who benefits by learning from your actions and changing your behavior.

STEP FOUR:
THIS IS MY COMMITMENT TO CHANGE

Step Four is the final step in taking authentic responsibility. With it, you can demonstrate your intention to do things better in the future than in the past.

Take a look at how these four steps fit together. You said what you did (Step One) and stated what (from your perspective) resulted from that action (Step Two). Then you listened to the person(s) you spoke with to see if they agreed (Step Two, continued). When everyone was in agreement, you (to the best of your ability in the moment) shared what you learned from this experience (Step Three).

You may not have much to share in Step Three in the moments right after an offensive action. You'd probably do a better job of addressing this situation if you had time to think about it and gain a clear perspective on your learning. Nonetheless, whether you just took an offensive action or are revisiting one from the recent past, do your best to identify your missteps and give the others involved the opportunity to witness your expanding awareness.

In Step Four, you state what you'll do differently the next time this kind of situation arises (hopefully, *before* you act inappropriately). Ask yourself:

- How can I behave or respond differently next time?
- What do I need to know about this experience to avoid repeating it?
- How can I demonstrate my increased intelligence and clarity for having gone through this experience?
- How can I assure the person(s) involved in this event that I'm not a repeat offender?

In Step Four, you develop your wisdom. You draw knowledge and discernment from this experience, however difficult it may be. Ideally, you'd do this all the time, but human beings seldom have original thoughts. We usually live on autopilot, thinking the same thoughts and doing the same things as always. We fill our lives with repetitive behaviors. Although some habits serve us well, many would serve us best by going away.

You can easily recognize habits that no longer serve you when others take offense to what you say or do. Suddenly, these unconscious habits look like mistakes.

But, does that make them wrong?

Not necessarily.

Your mistakes are blessings in disguise. Right now, you may feel like an all-knowing, invisible, and stealthy presence within you has encouraged you to take an action that got you in trouble. However, instead of being a devil on your shoulder, this event may well be an angel that wants to help you see something important about your life.

Even if you're uncomfortable at first, there's a higher reality. This is an opportunity to rethink something buried in your belief system that doesn't serve you anymore. You can reestablish better behavior patterns that will pay off in the future. In these moments, you can wake up, pay attention, and create new, more functional behaviors.

Events that look like mistakes (the things you're confronting throughout this entire process) are really blessings in disguise. They're trying to wake us up so we pay attention. They offer us opportunities to change and improve our lives. In moments of conflict, we're tempted just to say we're sorry, make our apologies, and leave it at that. But if we succumb to these easy cop-outs, we throw away chances to learn important lessons and improve our ways of being in the world.

Mistakes are gifts, although it may feel like someone's given you a present that's heavy and hard to hold. Rather than realizing the value of this gift and considering how it might benefit your life, you're tempted to chuck it in the garbage.

The thing is, if you throw it away, someone else will soon hand you a similar gift. This next one will be a bit heavier and more uncomfortable than the last. You'll probably throw it in the garbage as quickly as possible (just as you did the first). But, sure enough, you'll soon get another gift—and another—and another.

At some point, these gifts will get so heavy it takes two hands to hold them. Your back and shoulders will hurt from the strain. You'll wonder if you can raise this object up high enough to get it into the garbage can. You'll struggle and strain but it'll lie there on the ground, and you'll stumble over it many times before trying again. Who knows how many attempts you'll have to make —you may never pick it up and throw it out.

Had you been willing to receive the small and light original gift, it would've helped you grow stronger and wiser. You wouldn't have needed the larger and more challenging gifts that came after it. But most of us don't respond to challenges that way. We prefer to dispose of our gifts rather than realize their value.

Perhaps you're ready to change your thinking about the gifts you receive. Maybe you can learn to accept your many opportunities to expand in conscious awareness. If you do, your life really will become easier, more enjoyable, and more meaningful.

So, what does a commitment to change look like?

It isn't too complicated. Just ask yourself what action you can commit to (instead of the one you just took) that could create a better outcome.

Here are some examples:

- I'll never say _____ to anyone ever again.
  Instead, I'll say _____.

- When I'm in this place doing _____, I'll pay attention
  and avoid doing _____.

- I'll do my very best to respect others' opinions—
  especially yours.

- I'll keep my opinions to myself until I'm certain of what
  I believe. Only then will I thoughtfully share what I think.

- I'll be mindful of my words. I'll make them more helpful
  and less hurtful.

- I'll listen more and not be so quick to judge or react.

- I'll consider your opinion before I share my thoughts.

- I'll do my very best to be on time from now on.

- Rather than criticize you, I'll try to understand your perspective by asking questions.

Notice that none of these examples involve blame or faultfinding—just better behavior. Don't try to deflect what happened
on anyone or anything else. In these moments, it's better to take
on too much responsibility than not enough.

It's true—we *are* prideful beings. We don't want to be told—
or have to admit—we've said or done something wrong. But,
being wrong is such a small and subjective idea compared to an
ever-increasing awareness of how our words and actions impact
ourselves and others. In a way, acknowledging our mistakes
makes us much wiser and more valuable to the world.

Everyone makes missteps. No matter what, you'll occasionally do and say things to which others take exception. Given the choice, I'd much rather be wise than right.

Which do you choose?

12

ALTERNATIVES TO SORRY

Now you have all the components to replace being sorry with a way of being responsive, compassionate, clear, and self-aware. Let me assure you, making this change in consciousness doesn't come automatically just from reading this book. You have to practice.

To help you grasp the functionality of this method of resolving missteps, I offer these sample scenarios. They cover a few of the virtually infinite ways we can err in our behavior, recover, and learn not to repeat our mistakes. I hope these all-purpose examples help you develop a more holistic understanding of this method.

EXAMPLE 1:

Bill sends out email invitations to a team meeting. Cheryl, an important team member, doesn't get an invitation. She walks into the meeting as it's ending and is clearly not happy!

Bill: Hi Cheryl. You're upset with me and have every right to be.

Cheryl: Yes, I am! How could you *not* tell me about this meeting?

Bill: You're right. I sent out the meeting notice, and you were not on the distribution. I messed up not only with you but the entire team. Your participation is essential to our success. Without you, we can't get our work done. Am I right?

Cheryl: Yes, you're right. Now, I want to be briefed on what happened and know my part in what you've decided today.

Bill: We need to address that as a team. But we first need to make sure this never happens again. Sarah, would you take responsibility for sending out meeting notices from now on? Clearly, this isn't my genius and I don't want to exclude anyone ever again. Will you handle that, Sarah?

Sarah: Sure, I'll do it.

Bill: Cheryl, does that work for you?

Cheryl: Absolutely!

Bill: Now, let's catch Cheryl up on our progress and hear her thoughts about where we're headed.

EXAMPLE 2:

Nancy's friend, Jill, is breaking up with her boyfriend. She comes to Nancy for consoling. Instead of comforting her friend, Nancy tells Jill that her boyfriend, Ted, is a jerk and she should have left him months ago. Jill begins to cry.

Nancy: Oh Jill, I just hurt your feelings. It was mean of me to say that about Ted.

Jill: This hurts so bad. I thought you'd help me through this. Instead, you just made me wrong for loving him.

Nancy: I know Ted's important to you. He's been in your life for over two years. I hate to see you hurting like this, especially when I've added to your pain.

Jill: I thought you were my friend—how could you talk to me like that?

Nancy: I am your friend. I spoke from my emotions without thinking. That's never a good idea, and I know better. Please forgive me—I want to be here for you.

Jill: I need you to be here for me right now. I'm feeling so lost and alone.

Nancy: I'm here for you and I won't repeat my mistake of stepping all over Ted. That isn't my place. So, how can I support you?

EXAMPLE 3:

David's being promoted within his company and tells his friend and coworker, Kevin. He specifically asks Kevin to keep this information in confidence because their company president, Mr. Elliott, wants to announce David's promotion at a staff meeting the next day.

David and Kevin join four of their colleagues for a beer after work. In the middle of their conversation, Kevin inadvertently mentions David's promotion for all to hear. David flares.

Kevin: Oh crap! I wasn't supposed to talk about that!

David: Damn right, you weren't! What's wrong with you?!

Kevin: Oh man, I was so excited for you I spoke without thinking. I just stepped all over our friendship. I'm embarrassed and don't want to mess this up for you.

David: Well, you *have* messed it up—and I'm really pissed at you.

Kevin: I don't blame you. I know this is a lot to ask of you all, but would you please keep this information to yourselves until Mr. Elliott makes the announcement tomorrow?

Jerry: Sure. David, don't worry about it, we've got your back. Right, guys?

Everyone: Right!

David: Thanks, guys.

Kevin: David, I know you're still pissed at me, but I want you to know I'd never intentionally do anything to screw

things up for you. I can't guarantee it, but I'll promise
—with all of these guys as my witnesses—to do my
best never to do this again. I mean it.

David: Shut up and drink your beer.

[Smiles all around the table]

EXAMPLE 4:

Gail and Brenda plan to meet for lunch at their favorite
restaurant. Gail arrives a few minutes early and gets a table. Their
agreed-upon time arrives, but Brenda doesn't. Gail sends Brenda
a text but receives no reply. She waits a while, then orders lunch
and eats alone. That night, Brenda calls.

Brenda: Hi, Gail. God, I feel so bad about missing our lunch.
          I had it on my calendar, and I just spaced out. I don't
          have a single excuse, and I feel just terrible.

Gail: It was hard, sitting there alone—not knowing if you
          were okay or if you'd just blown me off.

Brenda: I can only imagine. I'd never intentionally blow you off,
          but this is a bigger problem for me than you know. I've
          missed a couple of other important appointments re-
          cently. They were on my calendar, but I just forgot.
          However, missing lunch with you today is the last straw.

Gail: What do you mean?

Brenda: First of all, it means I owe you big time. Why don't you
          let me cook for you on Friday night? You don't have to
          bring anything; just come over and let me dote on you.

Brenda: Second, I need a better system for keeping my appointments. Maybe if I make it a daily practice of reviewing
my calendar every morning, I'll have a better chance of
knowing what's coming up. In a way, standing you up
today may help me work out this issue and make my
whole life work better.

I love you so much! Can you forgive me? The next time
we have a lunch date, I promise to call you in the morning and let you know I've remembered.

Gail: Okay—Let's do Friday night. I like your new plan for
keeping appointments. And, I love you, too.

EXAMPLE 5:

Bob and Cindy take a weeklong trip to visit relatives. As is his
custom, Bob asks his neighbor Pete, who has a key, to keep an eye
on the house. When Bob and Cindy return home, Bob notices
almost immediately that his PlayStation isn't in its normal place.

Impulsively, Bob calls Pete and asks him where his console is.
Pete has no idea what Bob's talking about. As Bob presses Pete,
both men get frustrated and abruptly end their conversation. At
that moment, Cindy walks in the room. Bob shares his upsetting
conversation with Pete. Cindy is aghast. She tells Bob that before
they left for their trip, she lent their PlayStation to another
neighbor whose grandchildren were visiting.

Cindy: I should've told you I'd done that before we left on our
trip. It just slipped my mind.

Bob: I wish I'd asked you first and hadn't spoken to Pete that way. Now I feel terrible.

Cindy: You probably should have asked me, but I certainly should've told you earlier. I promise to let you know anytime I lend anything out in the future. Do you want me to call Pete?

Bob: No—I need to call him back and clean this up.

Cindy: Well, if there's anything you want me to do, just say so.

[Bob calls Pete]

Pete: Hello.

Bob: Hi, Pete. We figured out the mystery. Cindy lent the PlayStation to the Jeffersons before we left town and didn't tell me. But more importantly, the idea that I'd question you at all has me feeling awful.

Pete: I don't know why you'd question me; I've always been a good neighbor and friend to you and Cindy.

Bob: You've been the best neighbor we've ever had. Dishonoring you by questioning your word is about the dumbest thing I could ever do.

Pete: Well, I'm glad you worked it out.

Bob: We've worked it out this time, but I've done this several times before. When something isn't in its place, I immediately think it's been taken. It's like an automatic default. Now that it's caused me to question you, I have to fix this part of my thinking.

Pete: How are you going to do that?

Bob: Well, I'll start by agreeing with Cindy that anytime I can't find something, I'll ask her first. If she doesn't know, I'll just keep looking until I find it.

Bob: I don't remember the last time anyone actually stole from me. It's time to start acting like it. It's also very important to me that you and I are okay. Your friendship means a lot to me, and I don't want my thoughtless words to get in our way.

Pete: No, we're good. Maybe in a few days, I'll check with you to see if you've had any recent robberies.

[Laughter]

Bob: And I'll deserve it.

[More laughter]

Human relationships and interactions never progress in straight lines. We all regularly miss the mark in our speech and actions. We say things we don't mean and do things without thinking them through. We need a way to rectify these missteps to maintain healthy and functional relationships. Being sorry isn't the answer. Honesty, transparency, and sincerity work much better.

In my experience, this method feels natural once you've done it a few times. However, don't expect never to say you're sorry ever again—you will. But, you'll find you apologize much less frequently. When you do, you'll catch yourself immediately and restate your intention—without even pausing to think.

There's one more bit of business left—identifying how *sorry* shows up in our speech and learning what to do about it.

13

LIVING
WITHOUT BEING SORRY

Reading this book has no doubt given you a heightened aware-ness of how often you and those around you say, "I'm sorry." So far, I've described the Sorry Syndrome and offered meaningful ways of taking responsibility for your life.

However, if you want to stop being sorry, you'll have to make significant changes in your everyday behavior. If you keep being sorry for the little things in your life, nothing will change. I invite you to join me in banishing this phrase and the burden it creates from your life—forever.

Consider these ways of living without apologies:

LEAVE A MESSAGE

Check out the message on your voicemail. Does it say, "I'm sorry I missed your call"? How could you be sorry if you didn't even know they'd called? All too often, customer service lines play recorded messages saying their companies are "sorry for any inconveniences." Some companies actually require their customer service representatives to say they're sorry at least once to every caller. That's insincere and inaccurate on so many levels! Consider changing your voicemail message to something like, "I can't take your call right now, and I'll call you back as soon as I'm available."

EMBRACE YOUR SHORTCOMINGS

There's no need to apologize for a pimple on your face, a spot on your shirt, not knowing the right word in the middle of the sentence, or anything else that falls short of the perfect impression you'd like to make on people. If someone comments on your pimple, tell him how much you enjoyed a rich dessert the night before. If someone points out a spot on your shirt, tell him you save a fortune by not sending everything to the dry cleaners. If someone chuckles when you can't think of *that word,* tell him you'll call him when the word comes to you at 3 a.m. That will keep the interaction light and playful.

IT'S TIME TO SPEAK

The next time you and another person speak at the same time, don't say you're sorry and keep talking. (Don't say you're sorry and stop talking, either.) Instead, just look at him and say,

"Go ahead." Or, if you feel it's your turn to speak, look at him and say, "I'll go first, okay?" He'll most likely yield to you. When you finish, look back to him and ask, "What were you going to say?" By doing this, you bring order and respect to your conversations.

INVADING COMFORT ZONES

When people get on and off elevators, they step into each other's comfort zones. This also happens in doorways, hallways, and myriad other places—often with a little bump. It's normal human interaction.

Most people say they're sorry in these moments, but why? If you recognize a person, step back and acknowledge their presence by saying, "Good morning" or "Hi" and calling them by name. If you don't know them, you can simply say, "Excuse me." Whatever you say, say it with a smile. Not being sorry isn't about living without manners or being insensitive to others' personal space. It serves us to be consciously aware of our language and always mean what we say.

RESPONSES TO GRIEF

When we first encounter the relatives and close friends of people who've died, we often say, "I'm sorry for your loss." What does this mean? How does it help?

Instead, you could say, "I miss (name of the one who's passed)" or "I'm so sad..." or "I love you." You can find infinite ways to express yourself meaningfully in moments of grief. Say what's real for you in the moment *without being sorry.*

We've all said, "I'm sorry, but..." when we don't want to challenge, insult, or hurt others' feelings. At the same time, we believe what we believe, we want to do what we want to do, and we want everyone to be okay with it. When you use this phrase, the word "but" implies that you really aren't sorry. Since that's the case, why say you're sorry at all?

Here are some examples of how to rephrase our language in these moments.

A Matter of Agreement

Imagine you're in a conversation with a friend or colleague. They say something with which you absolutely do *not* agree. What would you do?

Most people would say, "I'm sorry, but..." Instead, you can say, "I don't agree. The way I see it..." or, "That's not true for me."

You're free to use these honest responses because you're entitled to disagree with anyone. Don't try to sidestep the matter, come in under the radar, or start by expressing the immediate disadvantage of being sorry. Just say what you mean by demonstrating confidence and clarity. What a good idea!

Be Thankful Rather Than Sorry

You said you'd take out the trash, but you didn't. Rather than apologizing for what you didn't do, express your gratitude for the person who *did* take it out. Admit you didn't do what you said you would. Then look around and see what else you can do to help.

This action brings the sharing of chores back in balance—and no one has to say they're sorry.

Priorities

If you're like me, people will call or step into your workspace, expecting you to stop everything and focus on what's important to them. They do this without knowing your priorities or what's on your schedule. They just know their project requires you to do something. In these kinds of circumstances, many clearheaded people might say, "I'm sorry, but I have to do this other thing first before I can help you."

Being sorry doesn't change the fact that you have different priorities. You're not making anyone wrong by knowing what's most important or urgent to you. You have the right to tell them what you're going to do. If it doesn't include what they want you to do at that moment, that's okay. Even if they're disappointed, they'll be well informed about what's going to happen (or not happen). You, on the other hand, should have absolutely no emotional baggage about clearly stating your intentions.

Meeting Others' Expectations

"I'm sorry, but I won't be able to do that for you." This lovely, well-mannered phrase is usually a lie. First of all, you aren't sorry. Second, it's not that you aren't able. Wouldn't it be more accurate to say you simply don't want to do what the other person wants? Be honest and say, "I don't want to do that." Doesn't that sound liberating?

You may want to use a more eloquent response. For example, a woman I know was asked to serve on a fund-raising committee. When the committee chair called and asked her to serve, she said, "This is a wonderful cause, and I know you're going to have great success in raising funds to support it. However, it doesn't fit into my plans right now, and I'm choosing not to be on your committee. Nonetheless, thank you for honoring me by asking me to serve." This gracious response left no room for misunderstandings or for the committee chair to continue pursuing her. Well done!

If we go through life guarded and concerned that we'll offend others, we'll never find the freedom to be ourselves. We should never project any sense of defiance or meanness when we speak our truth. In fact, when people can rely on us to say what we think and to share what we feel, they'll become ever more comfortable with (and reliant on) our transparency.

The Right to Disagree

People won't agree with everything you do. They're entitled to disagree—and so are you. Everyone has the right to their opinion. However, even if you're completely comfortable with and steadfast in the way you see the world, you can still benefit from listening to others.

My reality is the sum total of my beliefs, opinions, and perceptions. The same is true for you. If you and I communicate our differences of opinion with each other, one of two things will happen: (1) one or both of us will rise to a higher reality, or (2) we'll become more resolute in our ways of seeing the world. Either way serves us.

Always be open to expanding your reality.

"THIS ISN'T ABOUT ME!"

Sometimes, people complain to me about things I did or didn't do, and I don't see anything wrong with my actions. It would be logical to defend myself, right?

Defending yourself against upset people rarely results in mutual agreements and positive outcomes. Some people think they can fix these situations by saying they're sorry. By now, you won't be surprised to learn that sorry doesn't work, either.

What does work is listening intently when people express themselves. Their upset probably has nothing to do with you. If you have the self-discipline not to take it personally, you may actually help this person get to the core of their issue. It takes considerable character to stand in the midst of someone's upset without judgment and encourage him to keep talking about what's going on.

In the midst of these circumstances, remember that if you don't feel at fault, the other person's upset isn't about you. Hold this thought, keep your heart open, and see what happens. The other person may realize he has unresolved issues that are ripe for healing. If you listen and seek to understand him, you could experience something wonderful as he works through the process.

WHEN OTHERS TELL YOU THEY'RE SORRY...

When you learn to recognize the Sorry Syndrome within you, you'll become aware of its presence in the lives of others.

When people say they're sorry, you could say, "Don't say you're sorry!" But this doesn't work—I've tried it. People don't want to be scolded or made to feel wrong. However, most of us are open to learning new things.

Instead try saying something like, "You don't have to be sorry. You didn't do anything wrong." This lets people pause a moment and realize they didn't do anything wrong. What a concept!

How others respond is entirely up to them. Some will say, "I know. I say I'm sorry way too much." Others will look at you quizzically, not knowing what to say. Occasionally, some people will say, "You know, you're right!"

I enjoy letting people off the hook by saying there's absolutely nothing to be sorry about. What they do with this information is none of my business. I'll just keep saying this to people as long as they keep saying they're sorry.

CONCLUSION

Please—step up and stop being sorry. Start knowing, seeing, and feeling the amazing presence you are in the world. You're a magnificent gift to everything and everyone in your life. Over the ages of human experience, great mystics and philosophers have developed this healthy self-awareness and achieved great senses of mastery.

DO WE CREATE THE CONDITIONS OF OUR LIVES?

We initiate our lives with every thought and feeling we express. To be effective, we must do this without expressing blame, shame, regret, or failure. When we're in conscious states of awareness, we learn from everyone we interact with. We know what works—and what we never want to experience again. We honor all life. We don't judge others—or our own experiences and circumstances.

WHAT WOULD OUR LIVES BE LIKE
IF WE DIDN'T HAVE A DEFAULT SORRY BUTTON?

To me, living in a world without *sorry* means my life is more honest, affirming, conscious, and meaningful. I want to live in a world where this is true for everyone.

HOW ABOUT YOU?